DAVID YOUNGREN

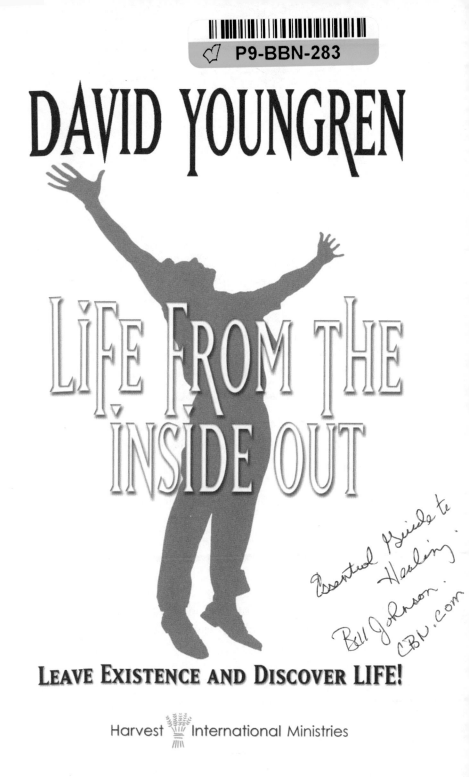

LIFE FROM THE INSIDE OUT

Essential Priusds to
Healing.
Bill Johnson.
CBN.com

LEAVE EXISTENCE AND DISCOVER LIFE!

Harvest International Ministries

Living from the Inside Out—Leave Existence and Discover LIFE!
©2004 by David Youngren

David Youngren
Harvest International Ministries
P.O. Box 37
Oshawa, ON L1H 7K8
Canada
www.davidyoungren.org

All Scripture quotations unless otherwise noted are from the New King James Version (NKJV). Copyright ©1979, 1980, 1982 by Thomas Nelson, Inc. Used by permission. All rights reserved.

The Scripture quotation marked AMP is taken from *The Amplified Bible, New Testament,* copyright ©1958, 1987 by The Lockman Foundation, La Habra, California.

All Scripture quotations marked NLT are taken from the *Holy Bible, New Living Translation,* copyright ©1996. Used by permission of Tyndale House Publishers, Inc., Wheaton, Illinois 60189. All rights reserved.

All Scripture quotations marked NIV are taken from *The Holy Bible: New International Version.* Copyright ©1973, 1978, 1984 by The International Bible Society. Used by permission of Zondervan Bible Publishers.

All Scripture quotations marked KJV are taken from the *King James Version* of the Bible.

ISBN: 1-893301-21-4

Dedication

To my wonderful Lord and Savior Jesus Christ who changed my life, and to Kim, my beautiful wife, and Nathanael and Sarah, my two incredible children, for their devoted support.

Acknowledgements

I'm so grateful to the many that have helped in preparing this book. First and foremost, my wife Kim. Not only did she help with the editing, but her words of support helped get this book started.

Without the incredible help of Dr. Larry Keefauver and his YMCS team this book would not have been possible. Their enormous amount of work has been a great gift to me and to the ministry. Thank you, Larry!

My son Nathanael has also been very instrumental by encouraging me to write this book. I don't know how many times he has urged me to write this book. Even when I thought it might never be done, his prodding words of support kept coming. Of course, I am also so thankful to my daughter, Sarah, who has had to sacrifice so much for the sake of the calling of God. She is truly a great pride to her father.

Much of the teaching in this book came after having been to a great church in Bogotá, Colombia, where I had a fresh encounter with Christ again. The incredible revival and passion for Christ that I witnessed there I have not seen anywhere else. After having been there for a second time, I realized that fulfilling the Great Commission is not so much a method, but it begins with a revelation of the cross from which everything else flows.

I also want to thank my wonderful church in Oshawa, Canada. I had the opportunity to establish this great church in 1995, and served it as the Founding and Senior Pastor for almost nine years. Together we have grown. Together we experienced the joys, triumphs and at times valleys that caused us to move toward greater maturity. Your friendship will always be remembered and fondly cherished. Many of you also had an input into this book, especially the great staff.

Finally, I want to acknowledge all the partners and friends of our ministry. Your support, prayers and kind words mean so much to us. They enable us to reach the world with the Good News of Jesus Christ!

David Youngren
Ontario, Canada
October, 2004

Table of Contents

Jesus answered and said to him,
"Most assuredly, I say to you,
unless one is born again, he
cannot see the kingdom of God."

—John 3:3

1

Is There *Life* After Birth?

"Marie. I've never felt more alive than I do right now,"
said Dan. "I thought I was doing just fine while I was
single, but since we've gotten married, a whole new dimen-
sion of life has been opened to me. I had no idea that
another person could make such a difference in my life."

Marriage opens the door to a relationship with another person unlike any other relationship. Friends can be close. Family can be close. But a married couple is as close as two people can be. Adam understood that when he said:

"This is now bone of my bones and flesh of my flesh; she
shall be called Woman because she was taken out of
Man." Therefore a man shall leave his father and mother
and be joined to his wife, and they shall become one
flesh. (Gen. 2:23,24)

For Dan in the story above, a fullness of life began when he married Marie and they became "one flesh." He wasn't even aware of what he'd been missing as a single man. How could he?

He wasn't in a position to realize the wonder of a loving relationship with his wife.

As we explore the notion of life, many questions arise such as…

- What is life?
- When does life begin?
- How can life be lived to the fullest?

When Does Life Begin?

The question of when life really begins has been at the heart of many discussions over the past thirty years. Science has searched for the origins of life in the universe and in the living cells of plants and animals. Lawyers have argued that life doesn't really begin for humans until viable bodily functions can be sustained outside of the womb. Others say that life for humans begins at conception.

Though this subject is important, we want to take it a step further and look at what really happens after a mother gives birth.

A baby cries.
An umbilical cord is cut.
A doctor, nurse or midwife announces, "It's a boy!" or "It's a girl!"
A mother sees her newborn and counts the fingers and toes.

When a baby is born, we say that a new life has come into the world. But is that really true? Has a new *life* really come into the world?

Not quite!

This may go against everything you have been taught or believed, but the truth is that *life* doesn't truly begin until there's a second birth. Human beings come into existence at their first birth, but into *life* at a second birth. The difference lies in the delineation of two kingdoms:

- Existence, which is the kingdom of this world.
- Life, which is only found in the Kingdom of God.

What's the difference? For example:

> Existence breathes in air.
> *Life* breathes in God's Spirit.

> Existence copes and survives.
> *Life* conquers and overcomes.

> Existence cries out in pain.
> *Life* cries out in joy.

> Existence tries.
> *Life* trusts.

> Existence is a sentence to death in the world's kingdom.
> *Life* is salvation for eternity in God's Kingdom.

The Beginnings of Existence

Consider the beginnings of your existence. Why and how did you get here? You were born into existence because of your parents, and ultimately because there was once a man named Adam, and his wife, Eve. Natural existence comes through the law of regeneration.

I had a grandfather who was a missionary to China and another grandfather who lived in Sweden and became a cowboy in the United States. Think about it. Were it not for my grandfathers, or if one of my other relatives had died, would I have even been born? Were it not for your grandparents, you wouldn't be here today either. Our existence comes through somebody else.

Adam was the first man. When he was created, he had *life* with God and life on earth—life in the Spirit as well as life in the flesh. God told Adam that if he ate of the tree of knowledge of good and evil, he would die (Gen. 2:17). Adam and Eve disobeyed God and ate fruit from the tree of knowledge of good and evil, which did indeed bring death. Adam didn't immediately drop dead physically, or in his flesh, but he did die immediately spiritually. He no longer had the *life* of God, but he had a physical existence.

What does that mean? Before the Fall, Adam had a relationship with God in the invisible or spiritual realm of God's Kingdom that brought him joy, peace and righteousness. When Adam then died spiritually, sin separated him from God. Life was replaced by mere existence.

Adam became aware that he was naked. Though he had been naked all along, he suddenly realized he was naked.

Prior to Adam's sin, the center of his existence was in the spiritual realm. His physical body was just the vehicle in which his spirit was made alive by his relationship with the living God. However, when Adam sinned, his spirit man was dead before God. Thus, the center of his existence became his flesh, which caused him to realize his own nakedness.

We are separated from God through the sin of Adam. Therefore, when the Scriptures say we're born of the flesh, it refers to our spiritual separation from God. It refers to being born into existence.

The Truth About Living

The Kingdom of God is everything God is. It is the totality of God, the realm of God and everything under His rule. The Kingdom of God is an eternal, spiritual kingdom.

The Bible declares, *"For the kingdom of God is not eating and drinking, but righteousness and peace and joy in the Holy Ghost"* (Rom. 14:17).

Compare that to the kingdom of the world. There, existence is defined as simply making it through each day—eating, drinking, working, coping, problem solving and trying to make the next goal, quota, paycheck or sales commission.

Bios, or mere physical existence is not enough. Jesus came to bring *zoe* or the God-kind of life. Comparing these two Greek words provide an interesting revelation of the difference.

Both words can be translated "life." However, *bios* is more akin to mere existence with no lasting meaning, purpose or continuity. If all of life is simply a dash between one's day of birth and day of death, 1945-2003 for example, then existence has no lasting meaning. But what happens in the dash makes all the difference! Is your dash just existence or was there life after birth? Was there zoe? What the Bible calls being "born again" into the Kingdom of God.

John the Baptist makes it clear that unless *we believe in the Son* we *shall not see life - zoe.* (John 3:36). It's possible to have been born into existence without even having seen true life. Without Christ, we cannot even truly see the significance, power or pleasure of *zoe* life.

Fast Foods of the Flesh

Mere existence (*bios*), life in the flesh, demands food; not the living bread and water of the Spirit. In the natural, when our body is hungry, we must feed it. Often, we're tempted to eat high fat, high calorie fast food. However, the empty calories in French-fries, starchy fried foods or high fat hamburgers don't satisfy and provide only temporary relief to hunger. But junk food is only one way the flesh tries to get joy, righteousness and peace. There are other "fast foods" of the flesh.

Fast Food #1: Materialism.

People often think that more money and possessions will make them happy, and to some extent it's true. An infusion of money brings momentary happiness.

If I have nothing and then suddenly have something, I'm happy. I get a sense of fulfillment when I can buy that new furniture that I have been longing for and looking at for so long.

It's the same when I finally get that new house, or I buy a new car, or something else that's new. I get an initial rush of adrenaline and a sense of fulfillment, joy and peace. I often will feel good about myself and I want to show the world what I have. But, sadly, the satisfaction of new possessions is short-lived.

The problem with new is that its luster quickly fades and becomes dim. Go on vacation, for example, and see how quickly the memory of it is moved to the back of your mind, even though you had a wonderful time. Sure, you felt happy while your flesh was satisfied, but it only lasted for a short time. The flesh is never happy for long, because the flesh has an insatiable appetite for pleasure and a constant craving for something new that will satisfy it.

That's why you'll always need something else that's new. Once you have a house, or new furniture, or a new car, you'll still need something else because new doesn't bring lasting satisfaction.

People are immersed in a never-ending search for peace and joy, and spend billions of dollars every year on psychologists, shrinks and counselors on their quest. People want peace in their hearts, and struggle desperately in the flesh to find it. Hence, the myth of materialism becomes one way that people search for satisfaction.

Fast Food #2: The false hope of religion.

Some realize that materialism is an empty hope and turn instead to religion, the other side of the coin. Religion is another attempt by man to find peace, joy and righteousness. However, unlike materialism where there is some fulfillment, religion provides very little joy. Any joy found in religion is fleeting and temporary.

In fact, religion is worse because it provides a false security of a life beyond natural existence. Religion is filled with rules–do this, don't do that. It's a man-made system of life we hope will make us righteous. However, religion cannot nor will not carry us into real living. We cannot earn or work our way into real life, no matter how hard we try.

The Crisis of Existence

Some people experience a "midlife crisis." They begin examining their life and come to realize that they haven't discovered what life is all about. Even being religious doesn't bring them satisfaction and their deepest needs still go unmet. The crisis comes because they suddenly realize that time is running out and they've still got so much to do.

Many respond by declaring the need to jump-start their flesh. They may have never exercised in their life, but now begin jogging or doing aerobics. These are simply futile attempts to renew and recapture their youth. They've looked in the mirror and noticed a receding hairline and wrinkles on their face. Now, hair replacement drugs or transplants become alternatives to looking old. Then, other physical issues appear—sagging skin, too much weight, low energy, etc. The realization that life is passing by makes them ask these ultimate questions:

- "What's happened?"
- "Why am I here on this earth?"
- "What am I doing with my life?"

These questions are simply the flesh trying to figure out the meaning of life. But it's impossible for the flesh to understand the realm of the Spirit. The kingdom of this world will never comprehend the Kingdom of God.

God speaks only the truth, which can be found in His Word, the Bible. However, religion lies to you; the world lies to you, and others in the flesh lie to you though it may be unintentional. Those in the world who merely exist may sincerely believe they know what existence is—but sincerity doesn't validate truth. Only God can validate truth. The truth is that the first Adam's legacy through all your ancestors is existence. However, through the second Adam, Jesus, you have the opportunity to choose *life*.

Are You *Living* in God's Kingdom?

The Kingdom of God is that eternal quality or eternal force that gives all of existence power and meaning. God's Kingdom brings an eternal quality to our lives that nothing else can bring. This impartation of eternal life gives us power to go on despite the circumstances that befall us. The new birth brings with it an eternal nature that ushers in peace, righteousness and joy into our lives.

Is your daily existence missing peace, righteousness and joy? If so, you need to be born again. Jesus said that you must be born again to see the Kingdom of God (John 3:3), and thus partake of true righteousness, joy and peace.

True *life*, *zoe*, is righteousness, peace and joy. But how does this second birth into *life* happen? Nicodemus wondered the same thing, so he asked Jesus:

> *"How can a man be born again when he is old? Can he enter the second time into his mother's womb and be born?" Jesus answered, "Most assuredly I say to you, unless one is born of water and the Spirit, he cannot enter the kingdom of God." (John 3:4-5)*

We enter the kingdom of the world through natural birth processes, because the kingdom of this world is natural, physical and of the flesh. However, God's Kingdom is Spirit. Therefore, to be born into God's Kingdom, which is Spirit, we must be born in a spiritual way.

Be Born of the Spirit

So when we draw the distinction between *bios* and *zoe*, we understand being born of the flesh only can produce existence while being born of the Spirit produces life:

> *"Do not marvel that I said to you, 'You must be born again.' The wind blows where it wishes, and you hear the sound of it, but cannot tell where it comes from and where it goes. So is everyone who is born of the Spirit."*
> (John 3:7-8)

Life in the Spirit is real life (*zoe*) and not just mere existence (*bios*). We exist in the flesh, but can live in the Spirit. Furthermore, without *life* we cannot experience true righteousness, true peace and true joy. We can't enter into that eternal quality unless we are born again, or become born of the Spirit.

Every person has an inner longing to be righteous, but it can't happen if we're only born of the flesh. The flesh seeks happiness and looks for ways to live in peace. However, peace, joy and righteousness can only come through life in the Spirit of God.

If you're like most people, you long to truthfully say…

- "I am righteous."
- "I have peace."
- "I have joy."

We've been born with this longing and therefore know that something is missing. Mere existence doesn't satisfy; we hunger and thirst for life. Therefore, our flesh attempts to manufacture some joy and will try to find the eternal qualities that only the

Spirit can produce. However, there are no shortcuts. Only one door leads to true life.

The Nature of *Life*!

But what does it means to be dead spiritually? The spiritually dead person is unresponsive to God, and is unaware that they are untouched by the life of God—His love, His mercy, His grace. The spiritually dead are alienated from the life of God and from all that God is. The spiritually dead exist, but do not have the *life* of God in them.

When Jesus told the story about the prodigal son, He defined death. After the prodigal son had left his father's house and traveled to a far country, he returned again. The father then said, "For **this my son was dead** and is alive again; he was lost and is found…" (Luke 15:24).

Although the son was not dead by our definition, according to Jesus he was dead because he was separated from his father. He was unaware and untouched by his father's love.

Using the analogy of human and dog life is another example which defines the difference between spiritual death and life, existence and life. A dog may seek the friendship of a human; it may imitate and even seek to please his master, but no matter how hard the dog tries, it will never become human. It does exist, but it does not have human life.

Religion is like the attempt of the dog to become human. It seeks to improve this dead, fleshly existence by imposing requirements or laws that imitate divine righteousness and purity.

However, it doesn't matter what we do, because we'll eventually fail. Only God can give us His life. We are born in the flesh, not in the Spirit.

Religion tries to describe what life in God is like. But how can you describe something you don't have? If you are dead to the life of God, you can't describe or begin to understand what the life of God is like.

The True Source of *Life*

This choice of life springs from God's desire to bring people back into relationship with Him. Existence in the flesh is passed from generation to generation beginning with Adam. However, life in God must be given birth—it has to start somewhere. Therefore, God sent His only Son, Jesus, to usher in this newness of life. Through Him, people can receive new life by choosing the life of God, the *zoe* kind of life. *Zoe* enables people to have that internal quality that brings joy, peace and righteousness; a quality that is not dependent upon circumstances nor moved by what is seen, but is only moved by the Word of God.

Scripture declares that death came through one man, Adam (Rom. 5:12). Likewise, life in God has come through one man, Jesus Christ (Rom. 5:15). Therefore, we do not serve a religion; we serve the living God of the Universe, Jesus Christ.

The Bible says that the life of the creature is in the blood (Lev. 17:11). Furthermore, we know through science that blood type is determined by the father and passed on to the offspring. Therefore, because Jesus was conceived by the Holy Spirit and not through natural relations between a man and a woman, His blood was that of the Father. Jesus literally had the blood of the

Father flowing through Him. Because God is holy and sinless, Jesus was sinless as well. He walked on this earth as the sinless Lamb of God.

Jesus came to handle the effect of Adam's sin. In other words, Jesus came to overcome both sin and the death that results from it by bearing it upon Himself on the cross at Calvary.

Jesus Endured the Cross

Though Jesus lived a completely sinless life, when the entire weight of the sins of humanity past, present and future were placed upon Him, Jesus felt completely alone. So alone, in fact, that He cried out to the Father, *"My God, My God, why have You forsaken Me?"* (Matt. 27:46).

As the Son of Man, Jesus had never felt the weight of sin, let alone its penalty. Nevertheless, God proved Himself faithful. When Jesus cried out to God the Father, He heard.

Jesus felt completely separated, unaware and unresponsive to the love, nearness and closeness of God. However, when He rose from the dead, He came forth in spiritual life. This truth is illustrated in Hebrews 2:9: *"Jesus…suffered death, so that by the grace of God he might taste death for everyone"* (NIV).

Jesus gave His life so He could bring all of humanity into all that God is and into relationship with God again. Jesus died so that we could have life. Just as Adam passed on life in the flesh and death in the Spirit, Jesus passed on life in the Spirit for those who are born again.

However, Jesus is not the founder of a new religion. He is the Savior of the world. Therefore, when you believe in Him and He comes and dwells inside you, the *life* of God begins flowing through you. Furthermore, as His life begins to flow through you all of the blessings of God begin to flow in your life as well.

God's *life* begins to transform you from the inside out. Your soul (flesh) is being transformed, as are your instincts, behaviors and habits. All these begin to change because the life of God is on the inside. Best of all, it's free. Jesus paid for it, and through Him you have received it.

Life's First Cry Is *Faith*!

Babies announce their arrival by crying. Likewise, the cry of a newborn Christian life is faith. A human baby needs nurturing and nourishment in order to survive, as does a newborn Christian. So how do you maintain life as a new Christian? How do you maintain a life in the Spirit?

Faith connects you to the *life of God*. By faith you can declare that you trust what God says is true. You can also declare your commitment to follow God's Word and to do what God has called you to do.

Think of it this way. You have a television, but with no antenna, cable or satellite dish, the picture on the television can't come alive. Likewise, without connecting your faith with God through Jesus Christ, you cannot come *alive!*

King David professed by faith, *"Yea, though I walk through the valley of the shadow of death..."* (Psalm 23:4). But what is the death he's referring to? It is separation, of being unaware and unresponsive to the love of God.

Have you ever gone through the valley of the shadow of death? This is a valley of life where you don't feel God or His peace or His joy.

Be assured, you will go through this valley of the shadow of death. Will you respond like King David did? Will you have faith instead of fear?

God seemed far away and unresponsive to David. However, the truth was that God was not far away. Still, David felt that way because he was going through the valley of the shadow of death. Notwithstanding his feelings, David's response was faith. He declared, *"I will fear no evil"* (Psalm 23:4).

Sickness may be knocking on your door. Financial troubles may be plaguing you. Life circumstances may indicate that nothing can be done and that God isn't there. Your family may be falling apart and countless other bleak situations threatening. It may even feel like death is coming upon you. You may even be wondering where God is.

However, like David you must declare in faith, *"Though I walk through the valley of the shadow of death, I will fear no evil; for You are with me…"* (v. 4).

You may not feel God's presence and wonder where He is. You may feel lonely and desperate and yearn for His awesome presence, but wonder where it is.

However, once you've tasted life in Christ, you can say with David, "Though I walk through the valley of the shadow of death, I will not fear these circumstances that are coming against me, for God is with me."

Life Puts on Christ

The Bible says that we must "put on Christ" (Rom. 13:14). When you become born again, you must "put on Christ" in order to maintain the life of the Spirit (Gal. 3:27). To put on Christ is to put on tender mercies, kindness, longsuffering, forgiveness and self-control.

You must put on everything that Jesus Christ is. In other words, you assume His identity, His personality. After all, you are a Christ-one, a Christian! Jesus is full of mercy and forgiveness, so put on His mercy and forgiveness. Likewise clothe yourself with His self-control, righteousness, tender mercies, kindness and longsuffering (patience).

To put on Christ is to begin living in the Spirit and allowing His life to flow through you to the world. Instead of being influenced by the world and the situations and circumstances that assail you, you're influenced by the Spirit of God and the character of Christ that dwells within you.

Ask Christ to dwell inside your heart, in your innermost being. He changes you from the inside out, moving you from mere existence to *life!*

> *Lord Jesus, I surrender my existence and die to myself. I ask You to forgive my sins. Live in me. Give me Your life. Thank You for dying for me so that I might live forever with You. Amen.*

You have let go of the commands of God and are holding on to the traditions of men.

—Mark 7:8 (NIV)

Chapter

2

You Choose: Religious Existence or Life's Good News

"Church really seemed dry and lifeless today, Sarah. What's the problem? Does it seem like we're hearing more about rules than about Jesus? Are you okay with what's happening?"

"I don't know what to think either, Mike. Pastor was really wound up about how some of the kids are dressing and wearing their hair. I didn't think it was as bad as he says, but maybe I'm wrong."

"Shouldn't we be feeling better after church instead of being drained and tired? I thought church was supposed to encourage us instead of beat us down. Is this all there is?"

Mike and Sarah are not unique. Their situation is played out countless times around the world as the church pushes religion instead of relationship. What are the root and the solution to lifeless religion?

Rules, Rules, Rules

The Gospel of Jesus Christ is not a list of rules to which one must adhere in order to find favor with God. Rules and regulations don't make a person righteous, only the blood of Jesus can do that.

Religion is made by man and filled with rules that prescribe righteous behavior. All a religious one has to do is check his behavior by the rules to see if he has fulfilled the righteous requirements of the law.

Jesus confronted this problem in His dealings with the Pharisees of His day. Because Jesus wasn't of their kind or educated in their schools, He was on the outside. Furthermore, Jesus didn't place emphasis on the same aspects of the law the Pharisees did. Therefore, to them He was a heretic, a blasphemer of God and not a true adherent to the religion of Israel.

Religion Binds—The Gospel Frees

Consider the consequences of religion. Jesus didn't adhere to the religious interpretation of God's Law so the heads of that religion sought His life. They would rather kill the embodiment of the Law instead of receive from Him the truth of the Law they served.

A vast gulf separates religion and the Gospel, so we must refuse to become religious people. Religion creates heavy burdens and great pain. Jesus came to set us free…

Then Jesus prayed this prayer: "O Father, Lord of heaven and earth, thank you for hiding the truth from those who think themselves so wise and clever, and for revealing it to the childlike. Yes, Father, it pleased you to do it this way!

"My Father has given me authority over everything. No one really knows the Son except the Father, and no one really knows the Father except the Son and those to whom the Son chooses to reveal him." (Matt. 11:25-27 NLT)

When Jesus called to the Father, He was talking about God the Father, Creator of the Universe. Jesus declared that we couldn't know the Father except through Himself, and that He chose those to whom He would reveal the Father.

Then Jesus said, "Come to me, all of you who are weary and carry heavy burdens, and I will give you rest. Take my yoke upon you. Let me teach you, because I am humble and gentle, and you will find rest for your souls. For my yoke fits perfectly, and the burden I give you is light." (Matt. 11:28-30 NLT)

I Will Give You Rest

Jesus said, "Come to me" to all who are burdened and weary and He will give rest for the soul. Thorough study of the context of these words helps us understand that Jesus was declaring war against religion. His words are not simply nice, encouraging words. This is a declaration of war against the very thing that causes people to become weary and burdened.

If you come to Jesus and know Him, you will know God the Father, which will give you rest. Then, the burdens of the world become light and their yoke easy.

The Pharisees had taken the yoke of the Law upon themselves, which was the heavy burden to which Jesus was referring. Picture two oxen that are yoked together, struggling under the load. This is how the Pharisees interpreted the Law and how to live under it.

Religion seeks information about God, without ever knowing Him. Jesus offers just the opposite—relationship with God, which eases the burdens of this life. When we take the yoke of Jesus upon us, we're in one side and Jesus is in the other. This way He helps us on our journey by carrying the weight of the load.

Look at the contrast between the yoke of religion and the yoke of relationship with Jesus:

- Religion weighs down—relationship builds up.
- Religion has one carry all the weight—relationship shares the load.
- Religion drains—relationship fills.
- Religion judges—relationship accepts.
- Religion kills—relationship births.

Jesus Proclaimed Freedom

Jesus' ministry involved three major emphases, all centered upon worship of Father God. All three are found in the Greek usage of the word, *sozo*, and include people being...

1. **Saved**. Jesus declared that He came to seek and to save those who are lost.

For God so loved the world that He gave His only begotten Son, that whoever believes in Him should not perish but have everlasting life. (John 3:16)

2. **Healed**. Jesus ministered healing to countless individuals, a few of which are mentioned in the Gospels.

And Jesus went about all Galilee, teaching in their synagogues, preaching the gospel of the kingdom, and healing all kinds of sickness and all kinds of disease among the people. Then His fame went throughout all Syria; and they brought to Him all sick people who were afflicted with various diseases and torments, and those who were demon-possessed, epileptics, and paralytics; and He healed them. (Matt. 4:23-24)

3. **Delivered**. Jesus set free those who were oppressed or possessed by demons, or were bound up by religious rules and regulations.

When evening had come, they brought to Him many who were demon-possessed. And He cast out the spirits with a word... (Matt. 8:16)

Jesus used Scripture to identify Himself and to declare His purpose for being here. Many accepted His proclamation, but the religious leaders sought to kill Him, claiming that He blasphemed Jehovah God.

He was handed the book of the prophet Isaiah. And when He had opened the book, He found the place where it was written:
"The Spirit of the LORD is upon Me,
Because He has anointed Me

> *To preach the gospel to the poor;*
> *He has sent Me to heal the brokenhearted,*
> *To proclaim liberty to the captives*
> *And recovery of sight to the blind,*
> *To set at liberty those who are oppressed;*
> *To proclaim the acceptable year of the LORD."*
> Then He closed the book, and gave it back to the
> attendant and sat down. And the eyes of all who were in
> the synagogue were fixed on Him. And He began to say
> to them, "Today this Scripture is fulfilled in your
> hearing." (Luke 4:17-21)

God despises religion because religion enslaves people and holds them in bondage. The word *religion* comes from two Latin words, one of which means, "to be in bondage." The second word means, "that in which we seek to please deity."

Therefore, we see that religion is a state of bondage through which people attempt to please God. However, our attempt to get to God will always lead us into bondage.

The Root of Religion

Where and how did religion begin? To answer that question, we must trace the history of humanity all the way back to the Garden of Eden where Adam and Eve first experienced the destructive effects of religion.

Genesis 3 records the account of the fall of man after Adam and Eve ate the fruit of the tree of the knowledge of good and evil. This was the first sin of man on earth, and it sent a shock wave across the globe that is still being felt today.

How did sin first begin to be expressed? *"So he said, 'I heard your voice in the garden, and I was afraid because I was naked; and I hid myself'"* (Gen. 3:10).

God was looking for Adam, but because Adam had sinned, he was afraid. Therefore, we see that fear is the first word in the vocabulary of sin. Fear did not exist before then and was learned from sin.

Adam's fear of God was birthed in the suspicion and mistrust inherent in religion. Religion doesn't trust God. Religion teaches that God constantly looks for ways to harm or destroy you.

The command God gave Adam in the Garden regarding the fruit of the tree of the knowledge of good and evil was that if he ate of it, he would surely die (Gen. 2:17). Adam thought God was going to kill him because he ate the fruit, but the death God was referring to was the spiritual death that comes through rebellion and disobedience.

Three Expressions of Fear

Today, there are three primary expressions of fear that are most prevalent. Closer examination of each will help you understand the futility behind rejection of God.

Expression #1: Materialism.

Materialism is fear based on the false hope of satisfying one's deepest longing for God with possessions and satisfying the insatiable desires of the flesh. Materialism declares, "I will act as if God is not present. I will eat, drink and be merry and will live for today in the hope that God doesn't come calling." Materialism lives only for today and grabs for all it can get.

Materialism doesn't think about tomorrow or what the future holds, its only concern is today and fulfilling the passions of the moment.

Expression #2: Atheism.

Atheism declares that there is no God. This is actually a response to the fear that there is a God who really means what He says. The atheist has no hope for tomorrow, except that there is no tomorrow and he isn't in it. In other words, the atheist wants to be a vapor that, when extinguished, ceases to exist. Therefore, the atheist declares that what one does in this world, on this plane of existence, is of no consequence.

Expression #3: Religion.

Religion is afraid of relationship with God. It is filled with fear of rejection and unworthiness, seeking to please God through rites and rituals instead of face-to-face communication. Religion is never secure in its place with God and is convinced that God wants to kill the person. The hallmark of religion is judgment between right and wrong. Therefore, countless rules are the foundation of religion. To be accepted, rules must be obeyed.

The Law of God

Religion began with rules in the Old Testament. During their captivity in Egypt, the Israelites lost the wonder of God's presence and had no vision of His wonderful love and provision. They were slaves beholden to their Egyptian slaveholders. Therefore, the people had no idea about how to relate to God. They had lost their intimacy with God and needed to be restored to a relationship with Him.

God gave the Israelites instructions in the form of the Ten Commandments, but they were unsuccessful in rote obedience to the Law. They learned that the Law was perfect, but they weren't. Performance was the door through which the Israelites attempted to gain access to God, but were unsuccessful because of the righteous requirements of the Law.

The Israelites used religion in their attempts to please God. They had stepped out of intimacy with God but knew that somehow the relationship had to be restored. Thus the interpretation of God's Law and the endless list of things that must be done to please Him. They quickly learned that rules and duties were no guarantee that God would respond, and in fact, witnessed the continued weakening of their national status. Finally, Israel was bound over to captivity and led away as prisoners of a conquering army.

Religion had let the people down and contributed to the captivity they now faced. One escape was in their past. Could there be another? If so, it would only come out of relationship.

The Façade of Religion

Religion constructs a false front that manifests when we don the Jesus smile or the Jesus mask. This condescending façade regularly compares itself with others to see how it measures up. "I'm better than you because..." or "Look at how well I'm obeying the rules."

When we come to church and compare ourselves to others we fall into the sewer of religion. When we critically examine what the elders are or aren't doing, religion has raised its ugly head. If we place the cell group leaders under scrutiny to pick apart what they do, or criticize the pastors, we've invited the hypocrisy of religion to rule in our lives.

Proverbs 14:12 declares, *"There is a way that seems right to a man, but its end is the way of death."* When religion creeps into the church, the life is sucked right out of it. Likewise, religion sucks the life and joy out of people. Religion takes away the reason why we worship God and steals the joy we have in lifting our hands.

The Good News of God

The Gospel is good news! The word *good* means, "whatever makes you leap for joy." The Gospel, or good news, ought to make you leap for joy because you understand it's *not* about what you have or haven't done!

News implies that something has happened. If you read the newspaper or watch news on television, you'll see what has happened that day. News is about the past and what already has taken place.

Religion reaches up to find God, but the Gospel reaches down to find people. Religion talks about what has happened and what we must do. However, the Gospel is what Jesus has already done for us on the cross two thousand years ago. Jesus demonstrated His love for us, regardless of how we act or what we do and regardless of what happens tomorrow. Jesus gave Himself so we could know love.

God so loved the world that He gave his only begotten Son (John 3:16). Jesus declared, *"It is finished"* on the cross (John 19:30). Therefore, we don't have to strive anymore! We simply need to come to Jesus! No longer must we look at ourselves and think we aren't good enough.

Because of Jesus, you can simply say, "God, I come to You. I'm full of wickedness, but You are changing my heart! Jesus now lives inside of me and the love of God has been shed abroad in my heart. I can stand firm in faith knowing that my Redeemer lives!" The Gospel of Jesus Christ declares it is done!

Set Free from Religious Formulas

Religion takes the things of God and turns them into meaning-less rituals. Then, the rituals are elevated to forms of worship. Sadly, the communion of the Lord's Supper has become one of those rituals. Instead of partaking in a beautiful meal in memory of our Lord, many Christians are bound by traditions that have nothing to do with the meaning of the meal. The elements are considered holy and revered above the One represented by the meal. The bread is simply bread and the wine simply wine. These two elements represent the body and blood of Jesus, but aren't His body and blood.

Religious formulas seek to put performance in the place where the heart should be. If the right person can do or say the right things in the right way at the right time in the right place, then the right thing will happen. Sadly, these formulas are faulty and bring frustration and despair. God cannot be confined to man-made rituals and rites. Instead, we must look to Jesus, the Author and Finisher of our faith to see what we must do.

Jesus made it very clear that He didn't conform to the religious practices of the day. Yes, He went to the Temple at the prescribed times. Yes, He worshiped each Sabbath, as was His custom. Yes,

He obeyed the Law of God, perfectly. However, Jesus didn't follow the faulty interpretations of men. He only did what He saw the Father do, and only spoke what He heard the Father say.

Jesus' purity in His pursuit of the Father is our model today. We must not lower ourselves into the pit of religiosity in vain attempts to please God. Instead, we take hold of Jesus and declare that, "By His stripes we are healed."

Our best pursuit is in unlocking the Scriptures to receive the fullness of the revelation of God and His Word. The Word of God must be inside of us and must be such a part of us that we measure everything against it to discern its truth or error for our lives.

God's Word is sharper than any two-edged sword (Heb. 4:12). It enables us to cut away the unnecessary portions of our lives and beliefs to reveal the truth of God in us. We can remove phony rites and religiosity and replace them with the truth of God. This enables us to "worship the Father in spirit and in truth" (John 4:23), which is the type of worship the Father seeks.

Scripture Reveals God

God gave us the Sabbath so that we could have rest from the daily routine. It's okay to have a fun day of rest. During Jesus' day, the people missed the entire meaning of the Sabbath rest because of religious rules. God didn't give the Sabbath just to make us keep it. God intended the Sabbath to be a day of rest and replenishment, of fun and relaxation. God knows we need to have some fun to be strengthened.

The first and greatest revelation of God comes in the form of His love for us. When we are gripped by His love, we're held fast and find great fulfillment. The Sabbath rest is one view of that love.

God declared, *"I will put My law in their minds, and write it on their hearts; and I will be their God, and they shall be My people"* (Jer. 31:33). Jesus carried that a step further by saying, *"A new commandment I give to you, that you love one another; as I have loved you, that you also love one another"* (John 13:34).

The new commandment is love, the fulfillment of all the law. God deposits His love on the inside of us, making it possible to love God with all our hearts, and others like we love ourselves. We live this out by asking...

- "Does this demonstrate the love of God?"
- "How should I respond in love?"
- "What would love do right now?"
- "How would love do it?"

God's love frees us from the religious nature that insists we must do things only one way according to the traditions of men. But how does this love work through us to be released?

Love is not something we struggle to do on our own. The Holy Spirit loves through us. This miracle enables us to love the unlovely and touch the untouchable. Truly, God's love has been "shed abroad by the Holy Spirit" (Rom. 5:5).

Filled with God's Love

When a person first receives Jesus as Savior, the Holy Spirit comes to indwell them. Not everyone is a loving person when they first come to Jesus. In fact, many people have deep problems with love because of the way they have been mistreated in their lives. God understands this and makes it possible for them to love through His love.

When you hear the Gospel of Jesus, the Holy Spirit embraces you in love. Your relationship with God is birthed in love and because you know the sin that was in your life, you understand the benefit of God. You've been on the other side, but now you can begin to do your Father's will, which includes loving others.

Furthermore, you now have power to overcome the very issues in your life that kept you immersed in sin and ungodly behavior. The Holy Spirit strengthens the weakness you once had and you're able to withstand the pull of temptation.

The reason this is so powerful is because of life, *zoe*. The Holy Spirit is filled with life. He is life. Paul wrote:

> *For the law of the Spirit of life in Christ Jesus has made me free from the law of sin and death.* (Rom. 8:2)

And again:

> *But if the Spirit of Him who raised Jesus from the dead dwells in you, He who raised Christ from the dead will also give life to your mortal bodies through His Spirit who dwells in you.* (Rom. 8:11)

Religion cannot bring life to your mortal body, nor can it restore your broken relationship with God. In fact, religion…

- offers no power, only rules.
- brings no relief, only despair.
- cannot save, only destroy.

Power to Live

Filled with the Holy Spirit's power, we become a mighty force for good in this world. We are free to live according to God's Word and open to His power through the *life* of the Holy Spirit that dwells within.

Religion has no hold over us because we're free in Christ to be His sons and daughters. Sin has no hold over us because we've been set free from the law of sin and death. The world has no hold over us because we're the children of God and members of His household. The enemy has no hold over us because we have authority over him and declare him defeated by the blood of the Lamb of God, Jesus Christ.

Everything we have in Jesus is the result of what He accomplished on the cross. Jesus did it, so we don't have to. Because we love Him, we receive His embrace. We abide in Him, and He abides in us. We are joined together as one through His Spirit.

We'll discover how this relationship is lived out in the following chapters.

Therefore, having been justified by faith, we have peace with God through our Lord Jesus Christ, through whom also we have access by faith into this grace in which we stand, and rejoice in hope of the glory of God.

—Romans 5:1-2

Chapter

3

Living From the Inside Out

"James, you're a Christian now, so it's time to ask the Lord about your hair," said Elder Simpson.

"Why?" asked James. "Can't a Christian have long hair? Is God concerned about my hair or is it just you?"

"Why is your hair long, James? Have you asked the Holy Spirit about it? Just pray about it and see what God shows you. You may be surprised at what you learn."

The essence of the Gospel is demonstrated in the life we have in God and what He has done for us, because it is God who lives inside us. Paul's letter to Titus provides a description of the lifestyle of the believer:

For the grace of God has been revealed, bringing salvation to all people. And we are instructed to turn from godless living and sinful pleasures. We should live in this evil world with self-control, right conduct, and devotion to God, while we look forward to that wonderful event when the glory of our great God and Savior, Jesus Christ, will be revealed. He gave his life to free us from every kind of sin, to cleanse us, and to make us his very own people, totally committed to doing what is right. (Titus 2:11-14 NLT)

Many religions have similar instructions because religion says we must not live according to the passions of the world. Instead, we are expected to live a good life and do good works.

Love Compels Us Toward Godliness

However, we are not a religious people. We have a relationship with God and are His sons and daughters. We have goals in our relationship with God that aim us toward rejecting ungodliness and living lives that are...

- godly
- righteous
- sober

This relationship is based on love—God's love for us and our love for Him—to the point where we become zealous in doing good works, eager to do what God asks. We want to do it because of our love for Him, not because we are forced. God's love draws us to church and to prayer, to study His Word and to tithe. We're called to witness and win souls, to share the Gospel of Jesus Christ and make disciples. God's plan for us is to live godly lives.

Sadly, many Christians seem reluctant when asked to do something for God. Often, this is because people have fallen for the temptation to try in their own strength and ability to do good works. They feel like they have to...

- attend church
- put on their best clothes
- lift their hands in worship to God
- read the Word of God more at home
- pray

They've become zealous after religion, not zealous for relationship with God.

Falling Victim to Religious Rigor

People often lack zealousness for God because of trying to live a self-disciplined, religious life, which is the reason many abandon their spiritual journey. They feel as if they can't do it so they just give up. Others attempt their own religious discipline through self-discipline, which involves efforts to control one's behavior by working on the outside rather than the inside.

During Jesus' day, the Pharisees were the most religious group of their time. Boys were raised from infants to become Pharisees. By the age of four, these children had memorized the entire book of Leviticus. By the age of twelve, these boys had entirely memorized the first five books in the Old Testament. When they reached their twentieth birthday they had also memorized the Psalms and the prophets.

Pharisees didn't just tithe their monetary income, but even tithed the number of leaves on the trees in their gardens! Outwardly, the Pharisees were doing the right thing, but not according to Jesus:

Woe to you, scribes and Pharisees, hypocrites! For you cleanse the outside of the cup and dish, but inside they are full of extortion and self-indulgence. (Matt. 23:25)

Self-disciplined religion prescribes rules to follow in order to be acceptable. Are we any different than the Pharisees of Jesus' day? Out of duty we religiously follow the rules, doing this and not doing that. In trying to outwardly conform, we pray, but have no idea what was prayed. Out of obligation, we put in our ten minutes.

This work of the flesh is an attempt to control the body. In trying to overcome the flesh I use my own abilities and strength.

Diet Christianity

A familiar expression declares, *"God helps those who help themselves."* Though it may sound true, it's not in Scripture. Nevertheless, we like to think that if we do our part and have done it correctly, God will help us out. However, religion is what compels us to do all we can in the hope that God will notice our good deeds. This false hope goes further and looks for a reward for all the good things we've done.

The religion of self-discipline is all about *doing*; about what I can do to earn God's favor and gain His recognition, thus earning His blessing.

This can be illustrated by what I call becoming a "Diet Christian." Many diets begin with a New Year's resolution to eat less in order to lose weight, so the person goes on a diet.

One diet regimen prohibits the consumption of sugar. So the person stops eating sugar and might even survive for an entire year! They think that discipline of the body is the key, and are able do it with sheer willpower for about a year. Then, after a taste of sugar, it's over.

Religion is like someone on a diet, trying to overcome their bad habits, or their excessive weight problem. They work hard at it for many months, even years, but most people are not able to maintain a strict diet. They often fall back into eating sugar again or eating wrong food which leads to gaining back their weight, because the most drastic chastening of the flesh cannot be kept up.

Religion gives us a detailed spiritual diet plan of rules and restrictions—trying to correct destructive habits and overcome sin, but since we are so addicted to sin, we cannot keep up the strict rules forever. For a period of time, we have some success, but eventually because it is an attempt on our part, our best intentions turn into failures. Like a diet, religion cannot make a long-term change in our lives. We need help!

Even pastors often fall prey to religion and establish structures within the church that attempt to dictate to the congregation what they need to do. It's burdensome to the people if laws and regulations must be adhered to in order for revival to fall and people to change. Religion only temporarily changes the behaviors and never changes people's hearts.

Our flesh wants to produce God's life on its own rather than depend on Christ to produce the life of God in us. Self-disciplined religion is independent of Jesus. Sadly, "Diet Christians" regularly fail; just like the vast majority of food dieters fail.

Law vs. Grace

Paul declared, *"For the grace of God that brings salvation has appeared to all men"* (Titus 2:11). The word *appeared* means "to make clear, to be a light in the midst of darkness." Darkness is dissipated by light. Darkness is similar to being in a fog. Once it lifts, you are again able to see what is around you.

Law is not the teacher. The grace of God teaches us. However, what is the grace of God? One definition in common use is "unmerited favor." *Strong's Greek & Hebrew Dictionary* defines grace as follows:

> *1)* ***grace***
> *a) that which affords joy, pleasure, delight, sweetness, charm, loveliness: grace of speech*
>
> *2)* ***goodwill, loving-kindness, favor***
> *a) of the merciful kindness by which God, exerting his holy influence upon souls, turns them to Christ, keeps, strengthens, increases them in Christian faith, knowledge, affection, and kindles them to the exercise of the Christian virtues*

Now, the Law came from Moses. Law is that which works on the external, the outside. Luke 2:40 states that the grace of God was upon Jesus. *He was full of grace and truth.* Paul wrote in Galatians 2:20-21 (KJV),

> *"I am crucified with Christ: nevertheless I live; yet not I, but Christ lives in me: and the life which I now live in the flesh I live by the faith of the Son of God, who loved*

me , and gave himself for me. I do not frustrate the grace of God: for if righteousness came by the law, then Christ is dead in vain."

Jesus paid for sin and restored our relationship with God when we could not. Paul said this: *Christ lives inside of me. Grace lives inside of me.*

God is love. Now, what is love? Love is the very essence of who God is.

Through good behavior and religious rituals, we try to convince God that we merit His love. But God's love and favor are not extended to us based on what we try to do. His love is not based upon the efforts or goodness of the recipient. He loves because His very nature is love; God freely offers His love to you and me.

Grace is the love of God in action. What God did to show us His love is grace in action. The grace of God is Christ dwelling on the inside of our hearts. Ephesians 3:17-19 says,

> *"That Christ may dwell in your hearts by faith; that you, being rooted and grounded in love, may be able to comprehend with all the saints what is the width and length and depth and height, to know the love of Christ...."*

So, the grace of God is God living inside through the Holy Spirit. Romans 5:5 (KJV) says,

> *"The love of God is shed abroad in our hearts by the Holy Ghost which is given unto us."*

Jeremiah 31:33 (KJV) declares:

> *"I will put my law in their inward parts and write it in their hearts; and will be their God, and they shall be my people."*

Jeremiah 31:34 reads:

> *"No more shall every man teach his neighbor, and every man his brother, saying, 'Know the LORD,' for they all shall know Me, from the least of them to the greatest of them,' says the LORD. 'For I will forgive their iniquity, and their sin I will remember no more.'"*

God's love is living on the inside. Ezekiel 11:19-20 encourages us to understand that the Holy Spirit causes us to do what our flesh cannot do. Listen with your heart. Understand who He is. Read about the love of God inside you and allow your heart to rule your flesh.

> *"Then I will give them one heart, and I will put a new spirit within them, and take the stony heart out of their flesh, and give them a heart of flesh, that they may walk in My statutes and keep My judgments and do them; and they shall be My people, and I will be their God."*

God will give you the desires of your heart. There is a flesh desire, and there is a heart desire. As you learn what is the heart's desire you have the Holy Spirit dwelling inside to guide you. Ask yourself:

- Am I acting in love?
- Am I doing what is right?
- Am I doing what God wants me to do?

The grace of God is teaching you to reject ungodliness and worldly lust. You will have His voice on the inside because that's a promise to the believer in Christ Jesus.

You will start losing the flesh desire and say, "I don't want to do what the flesh wants to do any more. I want to do what God wants to do." There is a struggle between your flesh and your heart. Your heart says, "No, don't do this." It was love speaking to you on the inside.

Now, love wasn't trying to condemn you or penalize you because you did not obey the rule. Law has to have a penalty to it. In order to enforce law there must be penalties. Otherwise, people will not obey the law. But God says, "Now, I am going to move on the inside of you. My grace is going to communicate to you how to live."

Stop the War Within Between Grace and Law

Finally the struggle can stop. I will not have to work hard at making a spiritual life happen. Now I can say, "God, I don't know what to do, but I thank You, Lord, that You have saved me, and I have been washed in the blood of Jesus. Sometimes I am struggling, Lord. I have these problems, Lord, but You live on the inside of me, and Your grace is sufficient for me. When I am weak, You are strong on the inside of me."

Continuing to let your body, mind or flesh control you is practicing cheap grace. People say, "Well, I am not under the Law. Therefore, I do not have to pray as much. I do not have to tithe. I can do whatever I want."

That is a misunderstanding of grace. Paul said in 1 Corinthians 15:10:

> *"But by the grace of God I am what I am, and His grace toward me was not in vain; but I labored more abundantly than they all, yet not I, but the grace of God which was with me."*

The greater understanding of the grace of God in you the more you will do.

In the New Testament there is not the same emphasis on tithing as in the Old Testament. But in the New Testament they gave everything; houses and homes. They gave everything they had because of the grace of God on the inside.

You now hear what love is saying and so you have the desire to give. To stop giving is not an option because you are motivated to give your life for others. Your heart has been changed.

I choose not to abuse my body with cigarettes or alcohol. My heart has no desire for it. My heart has been changed. Now my heart says,

> *"All things are lawful for me, but not all things are helpful. All things are lawful for me, but not all things edify. Let no one seek his own, but each one the other's well being"* (1 Cor. 10:23-23).

How does love work? Love operates by not seeking my own interests. The issue is not whether or not it is Law.

The Holy Spirit Empowers You to Live by Grace!

My motivation is to walk by love. That is what the Holy Spirit is producing inside of me. He is producing the fruit of the Spirit—love.

The goal of grace is that we walk in the Spirit. The method God uses to establish us in the Spirit is temptation. Luke 4 records how the Spirit led Jesus into the wilderness and He was tempted. When He came through temptation, after overcoming tempta-tion, He was full of the power of the Spirit. The purpose of temptation is not meant for you to fail. Everyone experiences temptation, opposition and attacks. Our reaction is to ask why these things happen.

These experiences establish us in the Spirit. In order for a plane to fly, there has to be wind resistance. Without resistance the plane cannot lift. Wind resistance helps the plane become airborne. Temptation, like wind resistance, gives us the opportu-nity to know that the love of God is truly on the inside of us and that the grace of God is really working. So we are going to have some problems and temptations. We are going to have struggles. We struggle so much because we are *learning* to live by the Spirit.

The power to overcome temptation by the Spirit. How does a religious person respond to temptation? He responds by drawing strength from the flesh. The disciple, Simon Peter said, "I will never deny You, Lord! If everyone else denies You, I will never deny You." He thought he could keep his promise to the Lord, but he found his own strength could not help him.

We are tempted to control and to suppress the flesh. The problem with our flesh is that we will eventually find a way to justify sin. It is amazing how people justify sin. They can find scripture or a verse to back them up and if that does not work for them, they compare themselves to someone else or someone else's situation. "Hey, look at them! They are doing it. So why can't I do it?"

When you begin to walk in the Spirit, to walk in the grace of God, to walk in love, temptation will come. When you are bombarded you lay down before God and say, "God, I cannot do it. I am overcome by the circumstances of life. I cannot do it on my own. My flesh is so weak. Greater is He who lives on the inside of me! He lives, no longer I, but Christ who lives inside of me. I choose to live in the strength of God."

Brokenness causes you to soar in the Spirit. I humble myself before God and surrender and declare, "I am trying so hard, but it's no use. I need You to guide me. I need Your Love, God, to speak to me." He responds, "I have enough confidence in Christ in you, the Holy Spirit on the inside of you, to teach you to live right, to live soberly."

Now you are soaring because the grace of God is abounding. The grace of God is on the inside, teaching you and instructing you, showing you how to really walk in love.

During the Jesus Movement in the 1970's many people out of the hippie generation met Jesus. They wore long hair and tattered clothing. Some had big holes in their pants. At one particular church the older saints complained, "We have all these people with long hair in our church." In those days it was called "ungodly" for a man to have long hair. People came to the pastor, saying, "You have to do something about these people with long hair. These guys are coming into the church and getting saved. They can't wear long hair anymore. It is ungodly."

He replied, "No. I am not going to do anything about it except I am going to talk to them. I am not going to tell them they can't wear long hair."

The pastor met with the "hippies" and said, "I want you in the next week to ask the Holy Spirit why you are wearing long hair, and then we are going to talk."

A week later they met again. A number of them sat together. The pastor asked each one in the group, "What is God saying to you about your hair?" One person said, "Well, God is saying to me to cut the hair." Another person responded, "The Holy Spirit is telling me I can keep my hair the way it is."

After he had gone through the entire room and asked each person what God said, about 60 percent of the people said the Holy Spirit, by the grace of God, told them to cut their hair. Forty percent of the people had received instruction by the Holy Spirit to leave the hair the way it was.

Was God confused? He gave different instructions to one set of people.

Then this pastor asked a second question. He said, "Tell me the reason why the Holy Spirit told you to cut your hair." 60 percent of the people, without fail, said, "The reason the Holy Spirit told me to cut my hair was because I was angry with society, with politicians and I was angry with my mother and father. There was anger on the inside of me, and I let my hair grow because I wanted to make a statement against society. I wanted to stand up and say, 'I will do whatever I want to do.'"

Then he looked at the other 40 percent of them and said, "So, what about you? Why have you grown your hair long?" They said, "Because we like long hair. It's cool. It looks good."

God is not as concerned about style as we are. If you like long hair, keep long hair. But if the reason why you have long hair is rooted out of rebellion in your heart, then you need to cut it. This is the grace of God. We cannot judge another person because they do not act and talk like us.

But we say, "I am going to teach you the Word of God." Teaching someone else the Word of God involves teaching them to listen to the Holy Spirit. Then they will know what to do because their hearts have been molded and changed by that wonderful grace on the inside, the grace of God. When the grace of God has changed your heart you desire to pray. You desire to tithe because you want to give Him everything. Let the law of God be written on the inside of you. Let your heart speak.

What if we fail? If we fail, it is because we forgot to trust Him. God continues to love us. The grace of God is full of compassion and mercy. God has only your best interest in mind. He is not trying to hit you over the head, but He wants you to be free.

When you are free, you have joy, peace and everything that God has. You have the blessings of God. That's why the grace of God is never easy on sin. Sin will often have consequences. These consequences are not there to punish us, but to bring us into freedom and victory in Christ.

Without the grace of God confronting sin, we more often than not would fall back into the same trap over and over and over again. So the grace of God allows consequences to set us back for a period of time in order to become less reliant on the flesh, and more dependent upon His work in us. Sometimes we have to go through the same thing over again until we are free in Christ Jesus.

So how does Christ dwell in your heart? When you receive the love of God you begin to comprehend how much He loves you, how much He cares about you, how much He has done for you. The old *you* has been crucified. The old *you* has been put away. All the temptations of the flesh have been put aside, and the new man, Christ Jesus, lives on the inside of you.

He directs you. When you follow His voice and His leading, you are safe. You are secure. You walk in the blessings of God. You walk in holiness. You are purified in Him. You do the works of God not because of force, guilt or condemnation; only because your heart wants to do it.

Stop Trying to Be Better— Live from the Inside Out!

God does not need to hear our promises telling Him how we are going to live better lives. Allow Him in us to guide us. He will change your heart. Don't worry about it. He will change your desires if you receive His love. Pray this, "I thank You, Lord, for what You have done for me. My sins have been forgiven."

A religious person thinks, *I haven't done anything wrong.* He is deceived. A religious person says, "I can do it on my own." That is the deception because he cannot make it on his own. God wants a broken heart—a broken heart that says, "God, I need You."

Religion will give you a plan to be free from sin. You will try so hard to be good and to do the right thing. You will try to discipline yourself, go to church and do what is right. But, you will keep failing because religion will never get you to God. But when you come to God, through Jesus, you are changed the moment your life begins in Him. God is not fair. He forgives every person the same. If you are the worst sinner on the face of the earth He forgives you.

God says, "I love you. Let Me take you and change you by My grace, by My love. Let Me transform you from the inside out."

Father, I repent of trying to change myself from the outside in...Change me, Lord, from the inside out! Amen.

For this reason I bow my knees to the Father of our Lord Jesus Christ, from whom the whole family in heaven and earth is named, that He would grant you, according to the riches of His glory, to be strengthened with might through His Spirit in the inner man, that Christ may dwell in your hearts through faith; that you, being rooted and grounded in love, may be able to comprehend with all the saints what is the width and length and depth and height—to know the love of Christ which passes knowledge; that you may be filled with all the fullness of God. Now to Him who is able to do exceedingly abundantly above all that we ask or think, according to the power that works in us, to Him be glory in the church by Christ Jesus to all generations, forever and ever. Amen.

—Eph. 3:14-21

Chapter

4

Christ's Life Indwelling You

"Daddy. I just want to be with you."

"But we've already had our story time, Honey. It's time for bed."

"I know, Daddy, but I just want to be with you. Will you tell me another story?"

How could I resist? My daughter's love pursued me and completely drew me in. "Okay, little one. I'll tell you another story. Come sit on my lap and help me find just the right one."

We often miss the meaning of the core of God's Word, which is the Gospel. Paul, while praying for the church in Ephesus, declared that the key to life is having Christ in your heart (Eph. 3:14-21). This key unlocks the answers to every problem of life and every circumstance one could face.

Religion will often try to change circumstances through laws, rules, regulations or legislation. Religious legalism thinks that if enough laws are introduced, people will change. But that's simply not true.

In fact, two very important issues affecting our society, abortion and same-sex marriage, are causing the church to look at changing the laws of our nation. While we believe that abortion is a sin and that marriage is between one man and one woman for life, how should we take a stand for truth and righteousness? Will simply changing the laws of the nation change the hearts of people?

While it's true that we need to have godly laws, a problem exists if the only emphasis of the church is changing ungodly laws. The fact is that every ungodly law could be changed, but people will still have abortions and homosexuals will still live together. Changing laws doesn't change hearts.

Be Filled with the Fullness of God

When people turn to Jesus, their hearts will change. If Christ resides inside, people are filled with all the fullness of God.

Being filled with all the fullness of God, means being full of all God is. Consider the holiness of God and His love, and you'll discover that…

- God is not a murderer, because love does not murder.
- God would never abort a pregnancy, because love would place value on the unborn baby.
- God would never commit sin, because love does not know how to sin.

However, is it possible for believers to not have Christ dwelling in fullness in their hearts? Many believers have experienced times in their lives when their heart became hardened. This condition isn't deliberately sought by Christians, but happens over time, often because of prayerlessness. When we're not in the presence of God on a regular basis, the fire in our heart begins to diminish and our love begins to grow cold and we become lukewarm. This happens because Christ is not fully developed in our hearts.

Religious Structure vs. Living Organism

Too often, the church stresses methodology or structure as priority while the hearts of the people remain unchanged. However, if the hearts of the people aren't changed, it doesn't matter how many witnessing programs are put in place to bring the unsaved into the Kingdom of God, the people will not respond and they will not become involved.

Many Christians attend church because the religious person inside of them tells them to. They want to ensure they make it to heaven, so they work to please God. These people think that by attending a church, raising their hands during worship once in awhile, and giving a little money in the offering, God will look favorably upon them and will accept them. This is nothing but religious structure, a routine of church attendance that accomplishes little or nothing on the inside of the person.

Many Christians don their Sunday costumes and paste on a Jesus smile to impress others who are just like them. They may be a grump in the car, but when they arrive and walk through the door, their religious mask hides their true self. They attempt to fool everyone, including themselves, but inside they're empty, pressed down by life's difficult situations.

These Christians are far from being filled with the fullness of God and having everything of God inside them. They are lukewarm and stand in danger of being spit out by God (Rev. 2:16).

The church is designed to be a living organism, dynamic and full of the life of God. As Christians, we're the church. Therefore, we're designed to be dynamic and full of the life of God as well. In fact, the church can't be filled with the fullness of God unless we are. We are the church! It's not a structure or a religious entity. The church is a dynamic, living, breathing organism, meant to fully express the Kingdom of God.

Possessing Love vs. Being Love

However, in order for our hearts to be changed, we must be rooted and grounded in love. When we are filled with the full-ness of God, His love fills and flows out of us. This love is not only for us; it's for everyone with whom we come into contact. Paul wrote:

> *That Christ may dwell in your hearts through faith; that you, being rooted and grounded in love, may be able to comprehend with all the saints what is the width and length and depth and height—to know the love of Christ which passes knowledge; that you may be filled with all the fullness of God. (Eph. 3:17-19)*

The Bible declares that God is love. Love is of God, because He is the very source of love. There is a difference between possessing love and being love. For example, I may have or possess some water, but if I give some away, I'll have less. That's what it means to have or possess something. However, no matter how much water I possess, I'm not water. I possess water, but I am not water.

God is love. His very existence is love. God is love by His very nature. Therefore, no matter how much love God gives away,

His love is not diminished. In other words, He will never run out of love because God is love. This is what it means to be love.

Paul declared that we must be rooted and grounded in love. To be rooted is to be attached. Therefore, we must be in Christ and attached to Christ in order to walk in the fullness of God. Likewise, we must be grounded, which means "consolidated" or brought together. This implies that our entire being is found in Christ, firmly attached and brought together in Him.

The Boundaries of God's Love

Paul wrote that God's love has height, length, width and depth (Eph. 3:18). However, is God's love limited?

God's love is far greater than anything we can ever understand, surpassing our knowledge and experience. God's love is not so small that He sprinkles it down on us from heaven. Instead, God's love surpasses our knowledge and our understanding.

However, the reason that the fullness of Christ is not dwelling in our hearts is because we haven't received a revelation of His love. If we have a revelation of the greatness of God's love and what He has done for us, our hearts are changed. First John 4:19 declares, *"We love Him because He first loved us."* However, if we don't know that God loves us and are unaware of how much He has done for us, then it's difficult for us to love Him.

Love flows out of having received love, which is God. When you comprehend the magnitude of what God has done for you, which is the width, height, length and depth of His love, some-thing happens inside of you. Your life is changed and you are rooted and grounded in His love. This is when God begins to fill

you with all His fullness. Suddenly, you begin doing things that
before you couldn't.

Beyond Judgment: Mercy!

Sadly, God is often portrayed as vengeful and quick to judge.
Punishment and wrath flow from Him instead of love and
mercy. However, this view of God is in error and lacking truth.
God described Himself to Moses and the Israelites as follows:

> *Now the LORD descended in the cloud and stood with
> him there, and proclaimed the name of the LORD. And
> the LORD passed before him and proclaimed, "The
> LORD, the LORD God, merciful and gracious, longsuf-
> fering, and abounding in goodness and truth, keeping
> mercy for thousands, forgiving iniquity and transgression
> and sin....* (Exodus 34:5-7)

God described Himself as "Lord God, merciful and gracious."
The Hebrew word for *merciful* is *checed* and is used 248 times in
the Old Testament. *Checed* has been translated as...

- merciful or mercy
- steadfast love
- covenant love
- unfailing love
- loyalty

Checed refers to the active expression of God's love, which has
three sides: strength, steadfastness and love. All of these expressions must be present in order to truly understand God's love.

The Fullness of God's Love

Common use of the word "love" often interprets it as romantic love. Romantic love is what people feel for one another. For example, a man and woman are attracted to each other and romantic love begins to grow. However, romantic is not the same as God's love.

God's mercy, *checed*, includes love that is defined as strength and steadfastness. This love is akin to that of a mother for her baby. Tenderly, she cares for her little one, even if awakened in the middle of the night by the baby's cries. This is an example of unfailing love, done because the mother loves with incredible love.

God's unfailing love will never let go, regardless of all the wrongs committed against it. It is a kind of love that doesn't push people away, no matter how much they've sinned against God. God still loves with a steadfast love. The story at the beginning of the chapter is one human example of that kind of love.

David was a man after God's own heart. However, he committed adultery and then murdered the woman's husband. Nevertheless, when confronted by the prophet, Nathan, David repented and cried out to God for pardon:

> *Have mercy upon me, O God,*
> *According to Your lovingkindness;*
> *According to the multitude of Your tender mercies,*
> *Blot out my transgressions.* (Psalm 51:1)

David had been discovered in his sins of murder and adultery, which the Law decreed should result in death. David, however, was convicted of his sin and cried out to God saying, "*Have mercy upon me, Oh God, according to Your lovingkindness (checed)."*

David realized that if he appealed to the law, he would be condemned and then stoned to death. However, he knew that if he appealed to the core of who God is, going beyond the law and beyond religion to the very heart and nature of God, then God would have no choice but to forgive Him because that's who God is.

David received this recognition from God because he understood something about God that religion can't. He understood that the Law was given to expose our sinfulness. David knew that everyone would stand before God without any righteousness because all are guilty. Thus, the Law revealed our need for Christ.

The Myth of Works

Many Christians believe that if they will do certain things God will bless them and give them a miracle. People will often ask me to pray for them because they need to be healed in their body. Then they'll tell me how sick they are, how sick they've been and for how long. Then they tell me that they've been saved for so many years. It's like a resume of what they do.

These poor folk are appealing to the Law that says they are condemned. They are appealing to religion that has already condemned them because they'll never measure up.

Very simply, you will never **earn** God's favor. There is no work you can do to earn God's favor.

Nevertheless, I pray for these people, yet when I lay hands on them, very often nothing happens. So they go to the next person and the cycle begins all over again. Round and round they go, like a dog chasing its tail.

These Christians don't understand that works don't accomplish anything. Everything that we have is because of God's loving-kindness, His *checed*, His love, His loyalty and His unfailing love for us. Yes. We tithe, we give and we do the things of God because we've received of His love. We are compelled to return His love.

The Promise of God's Love

The unfailing, steadfast love of God is in continual pursuit of us no matter what we've done or where we've been. The psalmist wondered, *"Where can I flee from Your presence?"* (Psalm 139:7) The answer to this question resonates with the *checed* of God:

> *If I ascend into heaven, You are there;*
> *If I make my bed in hell, behold, You are there.*
> *If I take the wings of the morning,*
> *And dwell in the uttermost parts of the sea,*
> *Even there Your hand shall lead me,*
> *And Your right hand shall hold me.*
> *If I say, "Surely the darkness shall fall on me,"*
> *Even the night shall be light about me;*
> *Indeed, the darkness shall not hide from You,*
> *But the night shines as the day;*
> *The darkness and the light are both alike to You.*
> (Psalm 139:8-12)

Likewise, Psalm 23:6 declares, *"Surely goodness and mercy shall follow me all the days of my life...."* The word *goodness* is *checed*, God's unfailing, steadfast love. You can't run away from God's love, so stop trying.

The Fulfillment of God's Love

Jesus is the fulfillment of God's eternal love. His love is eternal in the sense that it knows no beginning or end; it is boundless. Paul wrote that the love of Christ surpasses all knowledge (Eph. 3:19). So how can we know His love if it's beyond our ability to know? We can know Christ's love because we know Him, the eternal Son of God.

The *Amplified Version* records Ephesians 3:19 as follows: *"[That you may really come] to know [practically, through experience, for yourselves]the love of Christ, which far surpasses mere knowledge[without experience]...."*

There are different kinds of knowing. For example, before I got married I knew how to raise children and how to be a husband, not from practical experience, but because I had read about it in Bible school. Then, I had my own children. I soon realized that I didn't know nearly as much as I thought I did.

Having knowledge about something and experiencing it are two different things. In order for Christ to dwell richly in your heart, you must move beyond the mere knowledge of His love into the experience of His love.

Experiencing Christ's love can only come through a personal revelation of the cross. When you have a revelation of what Jesus did for you, your life will change!

I was a young man when I got saved. Though I was raised in a Christian home and knew things about God, I had no revelation of the cross and the love of God. Therefore, when my eyes were opened and I experienced His great love for me, I began to weep uncontrollably. Even though I felt like a miserable sinner, God loved me and forgave me. My heart was changed with a revelation of the cross.

That I May Know Him

Paul had an encounter with Jesus that changed his heart. He was a murderer and persecutor of the church. However, when he had an encounter with Jesus, his heart was changed, and therefore, his life.

Today, many people who attend church know about God, but have never experienced Him. Others who attend have lost their experience of Jesus. Paul was consumed with his quest to know Jesus. He cried out, *"That I may know Him..."* (Phil. 3:10). Paul's deepest desire was to experience Christ and have intimate knowledge of Him. He wanted to know the fullness of Jesus' love in his heart.

Some time ago I cried out to God and asked, *"Why is a heart so hard toward You? Why does it seem like being in church is just a ritual we go through? We hear the Word of God, but nothing ever changes."*

God spoke to my heart and said, *"Because people have knowledge about Christ and what He did, but they have not experienced His love. They have not experienced the greatness of His love so they continue to face defeat after defeat."*

I began to pray for change, beginning with me. *"Lord God, I pray that You would touch my heart."*

Encountering the Cross

I've experienced a number of encounters of the cross during my life, but I realized that my heart could still become hardened to the reality of the love of Christ. Therefore, I began to ask God to renew my revelation of the cross. Like Paul, I cried out, *"That I may know Him."*

Recently, I was in Bogotá, Columbia, and the Lord spoke to my heart about this being the year of new beginnings. God showed me that many Christians have become lukewarm and stagnated; they've become religious. These Christians know about God, but have lost the practicality of knowing Him in their hearts. So I prayed for God to give me a new revelation of the cross.

Three days later, a person stood in a service and read from the Word of God. While he was reading, the presence of God suddenly filled the room. Once again, I began to understand what Jesus has done for me on the cross two thousand years ago. Throughout the stadium, people began to weep because of this fresh revelation of the cross.

Religion or Jesus, You Choose

I don't want to implement any idea simply because it's a good thing. I want to implement it because God's heart has changed me. I don't want to preach something because it's good, neither do I desire to march against issues like abortion, telling people what they can or cannot do. I'm not interested in imposing laws, legislations and rules. I want to see the hearts of people changed.

I refuse to settle for status quo Christianity. Furthermore, I refuse to settle for lukewarm Christianity and petty religious rituals. I don't want to feel good about myself because I'm better than everyone who doesn't go to church.

I want Jesus in my heart. I want to be flooded with His light. I want to encounter Him. I can't get enough of Jesus, because I want to be filled with all the fullness of God.

When you have a revelation of the cross, your behavior will change in response to God's infinite love. You'll begin losing your desire to sin and will begin to witness to others and pray. You'll begin to do what God wants you to do, because Christ is in your heart.

What about you? Do you want religion with all its pride and hardness, or do you want Jesus?

I only want Jesus. Anything else pales in comparison to Him. People, my life, my surroundings, everything will fail me. I want Christ in my heart and want to be rooted and grounded in His love. I want to know Him intimately.

Look to Jesus, and see what He did on the cross. His love pursues you and will not let you go.

The mystery which has been hidden from ages and from generations…now has been revealed to His saints. To them God willed to make known what are the riches of the glory of this mystery among the Gentiles: which is Christ in you, the hope of glory.

Col. 1:26-27

Chapter

5

The Glory of Life in You

"What do you mean, Christians are supposed to be invisible? Is this some kind of science fiction stuff?"

"No, Jeff. What I'm saying is that too often, Christians get in the way of the world seeing Christ in them. They're so full of themselves that Christ is invisible in them instead of the other way around."

"How can a person be invisible, Sam? I don't understand."

"I'm not saying that your body is not visible, Jeff. But your body is only part of what people 'see' when they are in your presence. Your behavior, your words, your attitudes, all work together to paint the picture of who you are. Only a life fully submitted to Christ will enable Christ to be visible in these 'invisible' aspects of your presence. Now do you see what I mean?"

"I understand, Sam. Thanks for clearing that up for me. I'm new at this, you know, so I've got a lot to learn."

As a new Christian, Jeff had a hard time understanding what it meant for Christ to be visible in his life instead of him. Many Christians struggle with this mystery as they go through trials in their lives. Nevertheless, as you submit your life to Christ, He becomes ever more visible in you.

Christ in You

The Apostle Paul wrote to the Colossian church about this mystery that had been hidden from ages and generations, *"Christ in you, the hope of glory"* (Col. 1:27). He also wrote to the church at Ephesus and declared:

> *That the God of our Lord Jesus Christ, the Father of glory, may give to you the spirit of wisdom and revelation in the knowledge of Him, the eyes of your understanding being enlightened; that you may know what is the hope of His calling, what are the riches of the glory of His inheritance in the saints.* (Eph. 1:17-18)

The riches Paul referred to are *Christ in you.* This same treasure is available to you today. Like Paul, I pray that your eyes will be opened to see this mystery and apprehend the profound truth of Christ in you. I pray that you no longer live, but that Christ lives in and through you, making you invisible and Him visible.

One of the greatest men to live in the last century was Smith Wigglesworth. He was an unusual character, a plumber by trade and not the most polished person. Nevertheless, his relentless pursuit of Christ enabled him to do countless miracles, including more than twenty people being raised from the dead!

I once read how Wigglesworth told a pastor, "God just spoke to me and said, 'I am going to burn you all up until there is no more Wigglesworth, only Jesus.'" Then with tears streaming down his face, Wigglesworth cried, "Oh God, come and do it. I don't want them to see me anymore, but I want them to see Jesus on the inside of me."

Smith Wigglesworth had a clear revelation of the truth of Christ living inside him, and his life changed as a result. Likewise, when you apprehend the revelation of Christ living in you, your life will change. Therefore, take hold of this promise of Jesus: *"If anyone loves Me, he will keep My word; and My Father will love him, and We will come to him and make Our home with him"* (John 14:23).

Apprehending the truth of Christ in you brings power to live that non-believers don't have. Nothing can block you in accomplishing God's will, for *"You are of God, little children, and have overcome them, because He who is in you is greater than he who is in the world"* (1 John 4:4).

Crucify the Flesh

Sadly, few Christians have a clear revelation of Christ dwelling in them. If they did, they would act more like Jesus and be less inclined to...

- backslide
- act like a baby
- murmur and complain
- behave selfishly
- gossip
- cause division

The tragic truth is that we often see very self-centered people in church. Taking no thought of others, they shove their way through in pursuit of healing or blessing or prayer. It's as if they don't even know that Jesus lives on the inside of them. These people want others to care more about them and their needs than they care about others.

However, we must not seek what others should do for us, but what Jesus inside of us is doing to others. With a revelation of Christ inside us, we become less inward focused and more outward focused. Instead of complaining about not being fed, or about the brother who offended us, or that the church's programs don't fill our needs, we'll instead let Christ dwell richly inside us and allow Him to be the One whom everyone sees.

So how do we walk in the revelation of Christ in us? The Apostle Paul wrote,

> *"I have been crucified with Christ; it is no longer I who live, but Christ lives in me; and the life which I now live in the flesh I live by faith in the Son of God, who loved me and gave Himself for me."* (Gal. 2:20)

Paul obviously had a revelation of Christ living on the inside, which had been enlightened by the Holy Spirit. Therefore, he knew the first thing that would happen was crucifixion of the flesh and its works. Paul knew that to be in Christ meant that his passions and desires had to be crucified.

The works of the flesh are contrary to Jesus living inside of us. The works of the flesh can be categorized into four areas as identified by Paul in Galatians 5:19-21, including:

1. Sexual impurity
2. The occult
3. Division or lack of unity
4. Self-indulgence and the unrestrained appetites and desires of the flesh

Winning the War Within

Our flesh must be crucified or put to death. Paul wrote about knowing Jesus:

> *That I may know Him and the power of His resurrection, and the fellowship of His sufferings, being conformed to His death, if, by any means, I may attain to the resurrection from the dead.* (Phil. 3:10-11)

How do we conform to Jesus' death? We must suffer in the flesh. Jesus' flesh was literally torn from His body. Our flesh (sin nature) is so much a part of us that it, too, must be torn away from us. Therefore, we crucify our flesh by offering our bodies a living sacrifice to God (Rom. 12:1). Peter wrote:

> *Therefore, since Christ suffered for us in the flesh, arm yourselves also with the same mind, for he who has suffered in the flesh has ceased from sin, that he no longer should live the rest of his time in the flesh for the lusts of men, but for the will of God.* (1 Peter 4:1-2)

As much as we don't like our flesh to suffer, there must be a suffering in our flesh in order for us to cease from sin. However, because we love our flesh, we want to see fulfilled its desires and passions. Nevertheless, Scripture declares that we have to die. We have to suffer in the flesh in order to cease from sin.

Be Willing to Sacrifice

Crucifying the flesh means overcoming its desires. For example: A young woman meets a dashing young man. Though she is committed to the Lord Jesus Christ, this handsome young man sweeps her off her feet and they become emotionally involved. However, all is not necessarily well. One of the pastors may be concerned that the young man may not have a genuine relationship with Christ but is only using it to win the young woman over. However, the young lady really likes the handsome young guy because he has "potential." Blinded by passion and fueled by the flesh, she declares her love for him.

Passion cannot rule our relationships. In fact, though we love other people, our love for Jesus must be greater. Likewise, though we trust those whom we love, our trust in God must be greater. Here the young lady may have to be willing to sacrifice her relationship or crucify the passions of her flesh in order to live from the inside out.

Men and women in business make decisions every day that either fuel the flesh or crucify it. Is it painful? Yes. Is it worth making the right decision? Absolutely.

Gossip feeds the flesh unlike any other activity. In fact, gossip is like candy to the flesh—it can't get enough of it. Refusing to talk about other people goes against the natural grain of human communications. However, the Bible says we're a "peculiar people," which means we don't do what the world does. We're set apart and different. Our flesh has been crucified.

Step Into the Power

Do you want more signs and wonders in your life? Do you want to see the glory of God more and experience the presence of God more? Then you must crucify the flesh daily. Every time you're faced with a decision to feed the flesh, crucify it instead. If you hear something and are tempted to gossip, keep your mouth shut. Crucify the flesh. Remember, greater is He who is in you than he who is in the world.

You walk in the revelation of Christ in you by letting Him live through you. Paul wrote, *"I have been crucified with Christ; it is no longer I who live, but Christ lives in me; and the life which I now live in the flesh I live by faith in the Son of God"* (Gal. 2:20). Realize this. Once you are dead, you are no longer living. Instead, it's Christ living inside of you.

Facts, Feelings & Faith

Facts are not necessarily the truth. This can be clearly demonstrated with Scripture. For example: A doctor may diagnose a person with cancer, and may even set a time frame for their life to end. However, the Prophet Isaiah declared:

> *"He was wounded for our transgressions,*
> *He was bruised for our iniquities;*
> *The chastisement for our peace was upon Him,*
> *And **by His stripes we are healed.***"
> (Isaiah 53:5 emphasis added)

See also:

> *When evening had come, they brought to Him many who were demon-possessed. And He cast out the spirits with a word, and healed all who were sick, that it might be fulfilled which was spoken by Isaiah the prophet, saying:*
> *'He Himself took our infirmities*
> *And bore our sicknesses.'* (Matt. 8:16-17)

The doctor's report was a fact—the person has cancer in their body. However, the truth of God is they are healed by the stripes of Jesus. We cannot let facts obscure the truth of God. Facts are the fodder of lawyers, while truth is the manna of God. Facts must only be received and acted upon when they align with the truth of God.

Feelings are the voice of the soul or the flesh, the voice of the old man. If you live by your feelings, then you'll be tossed around like a cork on stormy seas. Feelings are neither true nor false, they're simply feelings. Feelings are expressions of the soul and methods by which we gain a handle on our emotions.

Never make a decision based on your feelings. If you make a practice of following your feelings, you'll lose all your friends and probably wind up broke and desperate. Why? Because feelings are not accurate barometers of truth. They are simply feelings.

Faith must fit into this equation. Faith is different than beliefs. Faith is unreserved trust in something or someone. This is why it's so important to identify where your faith is placed. Do you have faith in God or in your doctor? Do you have faith in your job or your Source, God? Faith is not swayed by feelings or facts. Faith is supported by truth and stands alone.

Now, let's examine all three at once:

- Facts are pieces of information presented as having objective reality.
- Feelings are expressions of the soul that reveal our emotions.
- Faith is unreserved trust in something or someone.

I must weigh the facts against the truth of God before any action is determined on my part. Any feelings associated with the facts are just that, feelings. I must not act on them because I could easily be led astray and deep into error. Faith is having unreserved trust in someone or something. Therefore, I must put my faith in the source of truth, God, so that my feelings come into alignment with truth. Likewise, I'll examine the facts of any situation against the truth of God and live my life accordingly.

Because I live through faith in the Son of God, I am not moved by circumstances around me. I am not moved by what I see and what I feel. Instead, I'm moved by what Jesus tells me on the inside! Therefore, it doesn't matter if all the circumstances in the world line up against me. *Greater is He who is in me than he who is in the world!*

To Africa by Faith in God

For years, we have been training and equipping pastors in many nations of the world. Often we have thousands of pastors come to our seminars, where we feed and accommodate all the delegates and even cover some of their travel costs. Many of them travel on bikes, on foot or on trains for days to attend our pastors' seminar. As can be imagined, often there are great costs involved with such large events.

A while ago, we again made arrangements to hold a large pastors' conference in Tanzania. After our good friend Elias Shija from Tanzania had done much of the planning, we realized as we looked at the circumstances, there was no way we could afford to proceed with this major undertaking. Circumstances were not lining up with what we knew we needed. I had to make a decision immediately, and I had run out of ideas to how we could raise the funds needed.

On the day that I was about send the cancellation to Elias, my wife said, "Well, God spoke to us, and God has said that we have much work to do in Africa. Are we going to look at circumstances, or are we going to look at Christ inside of us who can do all things?"

Her words cut right into my heart, and I replied, "Lord, oh yes, Lord. I will trust You." Two months later we equipped thousands in Tanzania.

We can't be moved by what we see. Instead, we must be moved by what moves and lives inside of us—Jesus Christ. When we choose to live according to Christ in me, it doesn't matter what the devil throws our way. *Greater is He who is in me than he who is in the world.* Therefore, every financial need shall be met. Not one pastor will be unable to come because Christ Jesus will meet every need according to His riches in glory.

You may not believe the miracle will happen, but watch and see the mighty hand of God at work! You must live by faith and not by sight.

Live by Faith

We must learn to live by faith in Christ Jesus in order for Him to live through You. We learn to live by faith in Christ Jesus and let Christ live through us when our flesh is brought to total weakness.

Paul wrote, *"For I have learned in whatever state I am, to be content: I know how to be abased, and I know how to abound.*

Everywhere and in all things I have learned both to be full and to be hungry, both to abound and to suffer need" (Phil. 4:11-12). The apostle learned that no matter what condition he was in, God was still in control and remained his source. Paul didn't depend upon his own strength or talent; he depended on God.

Paul discussed this in another letter, explaining that his own weakness served as the platform for Christ's strength. Paul had prayed to the Lord about a "thorn in the flesh" that bothered him. Opinions abound as to what was that thorn in the flesh. Personally, I believe that Paul was referring to the people he previously mentioned who had caused him much distress. Regardless of the nature of the thorn in the flesh that was a messenger of Satan, Paul wrote:

> *Concerning this thing I pleaded with the Lord three times that it might depart from me. And He said to me, "My grace is sufficient for you, for My strength is made perfect in weakness." Therefore most gladly I will rather boast in my infirmities, that the power of Christ may rest upon me. Therefore I take pleasure in infirmities, in reproaches, in needs, in persecutions, in distresses, for Christ's sake. **For when I am weak, then I am strong.*** (2 Cor. 12:8-10 KJV emphasis added)

When problems have no answer, we're forced to depend upon Christ who infuses us with His strength. He is on the inside, so when problems happen we have somewhere to go. No one likes problems, but according to Paul he delighted in problems because they caused him to depend on Christ within, rather than on his own ability, i.e., living from the inside out.

Problems enable us to stop doing things on our own, and let Christ on the inside do it for us. Remember, *"It is no longer I*

who lives, but Christ who lives on the inside of me." We allow
Christ to live through us by obeying His Word. We must obey
His Word so that the ability, the *dunamis* (power) of God, is
infused into our life: *"Now to Him who is able to do exceedingly
abundantly above all that we ask or think, according to the power
that works in us"* (Eph. 3:20).

There is a power that works inside of you, which is Christ on the
inside. Therefore, you are able to do exceedingly abundantly
above all that you may think or imagine. That's why, when you
begin to walk with Christ on the inside of you, an entirely new
realm of potential and possibility opens to you. That's the favor
of God.

Favor means that the provisions are coming your way. As you
walk in the revelation of Christ, you'll see the favor of God upon
everything that you do. It will affect the circumstances of your
life. When Jesus needed money to pay taxes, He sent Peter who
found it in the mouth of a fish.

You see, walking by faith means that you allow the Word of God
to control you. It is not really about your needs being met. It is
about people getting saved, healed and delivered.

Imagine going to the mall and the healing anointing of God
coming over you when you see a person who is sick. So you lay
your hands on them and they're healed by the mighty power of
Christ in you! This revelation changes you as you let Jesus rule
and govern your life.

So what are you going to do with this? It's time for you to look
deep inside and see the Christ in you. Recognize that the fullness
of the Godhead dwells in you in Christ Jesus. Therefore,
nothing can stand in your way. No problem, no circumstance,

no issue and no person can thwart the plans of God in your life. All you have to do is live a life of obedience to Christ. Sound difficult? It isn't. Pray this prayer out loud to unlock the mystery of Christ in you, the hope of glory:

> *Christ Jesus, I know that You dwell inside me. The promises of Scripture are true and I accept them as the guide for my life. Have full control, Jesus. Do with my life what You will. I'm Yours.*
>
> *Thank You, Lord, for choosing me. I declare my purpose is to live wholly for You daily. Receive my life in exchange for Yours I pray. In Jesus' name. Amen.*

No one will be able to stand their ground against you as long as you live. For I will be with you as I was with Moses. I will not fail you or abandon you.

—Joshua 1:5 (NLT)

Chapter

6

Preventing Spiritual Burnout

"I'm about finished, Phil. It seems like God has shut His ears to my prayers and isn't listening. I feel like I'm at the end of my rope with nobody to catch me when I fall. I don't know what else to do."

"I can see the stress all over you, Mary. But I don't think God has given up on you or this problem."

"Maybe so. I just feel like I've been hung out to dry. Will you pray with me for strength to hang on another day?"

"Of course I'll pray with you, Mary. 'Heavenly Father....'"

Mary's situation is not uncommon among Christians today. Surrounded by stressful situations and overcommitted at home, at work and at church, Christians around the world are wondering what's happening. They question God and even begin to lose faith in Him as their prayers seem to fall on deaf ears.

Is God really ignoring them? Let's look at this problem of spiritual burnout and see if we can gain the upper hand in preventing it from happening to us.

Have You Forgotten Us, God?

Israel strayed away from God many times throughout their history. Usually, it was because of prosperity and subsequent idol worship, but the end result was the same—captivity and bondage. Then, enslaved by their captors, the people would begin crying out to God, asking Him why they had been forsaken. The prophets would turn the focus back to the sins of the nation, which often led to national repentance and mourning before God. Then God would hear their cries and would respond in love and mercy.

Throughout the darkness of Israel's trials, God would shine a light on the future and His promise for the nation. A perfect example of this is written in the book of Isaiah, chapter 40:

> *O Israel, how can you say the LORD does not see your troubles? How can you say God refuses to hear your case? Have you never heard or understood? Don't you know that the LORD is the everlasting God, the Creator of all the earth? He never grows faint or weary. No one can measure the depths of his understanding. He gives power to those who are tired and worn out; he offers strength to the weak. Even youths will become exhausted, and young men will give up. But those who wait on the LORD will find new strength. They will fly high on wings like eagles. They will run and not grow weary. They will walk and not faint.* (Isaiah 40:27-31 NLT)

Isaiah is talking about the people who have a covenant relationship with God. He points out that God is not far from them and has heard their cries and knows their troubles.

What we see here is a classic case of "spiritual burnout." Like Mary in the story at the beginning of this chapter, the Israelites were questioning whether God was even aware of them and their difficulties. God seemed very far away for them and out of touch with their plight.

- Have you ever felt that way?
- Have you felt as if your prayers went nowhere?
- Have you ever felt like a failure as a Christian, unable to do what you're supposed to do?
- Have you ever felt like the harder you try the worse things become?

Most Christians don't want to verbalize thoughts like these. Nevertheless, they wonder where God is and if He really cares about them.

Limited Strength

Thoughts like these are classic symptoms of having run out of strength. When you run out of strength, you experience burnout. However, what kind of strength has run out?

The strength I'm referring to is your own mental and spiritual strength, which is limited. Overdrawing your spiritual and mental strength will drain you physically as well, causing weakness and lack of resolve. In this condition, you will be quick to question God's presence and are susceptible of dropping out of the race before its completion.

Drawing from your flesh in attempts to walk in the fullness of Christ leads to failure and spiritual burnout. In our attempt to understand this condition, let's examine the symptoms of spiritual burnout.

Symptom #1: Denial

This symptom is a dangerous prelude to greater problems. Denial occurs when you choose not to acknowledge your condition, thus putting yourself in even greater danger. Often, efforts to mask denial of a real problem are attempted by falsely citing "positive confessions," and declaring there are no real problems to be concerned about. However, true positive confession is birthed in faith and in the reality of "walking by faith and not by sight." Moreover, problems are always acknowledged, but are walked through by faith.

Christians in denial don't feel like lifting their hands in praise and worship to God, and don't even feel like being in church. If they do go, it's out of duty and obligation. Outwardly, everything appears to be just fine, but inside, they are desperately alone.

Symptom #2: Pulling Away

The second major symptom is when Christians begin to separate themselves from others. Pulling away from others may be a sign of mistrust. However, another reason may be that of viewing self as a hypocrite because of questioning God and thus feeling less than what a Christian "should be."

Symptom #3: Anger

Becoming angry with God is the third symptom of spiritual burnout. Christians wonder where God is and what He is doing about their problem or situation. These folk become angry at the church because it doesn't seem to care any more than God does. Then they become angry with the pastor, the messenger of the Gospel who represents God, and God doesn't seem to care.

Symptom #4: Bitterness

Bitterness leads to unforgiveness, which is a sure sign of a wounded heart. You don't know why, but you are unable to forgive others. People bother you. The church bothers you. Just looking into the faces of others bothers you. That something is bitterness on the inside, a sign of spiritual burnout.

Symptom #5: Sarcasm

Suddenly, everybody's motives are called into question and you become cynical about everything. Criticism streams from your mouth instead of praise. Nothing, or no one, is immune to your torrent of critical words. This is a sign of spiritual burnout.

Burnout to be Burned Up

Spiritual burnout occurs when you draw only from your own strength in trying to make the Christian life work. Burnout happens when you work to be a saint of God, trying to be holy and righteous, doing everything you know you're supposed to do. A sure sign you're burned out is when you read your Bible and see nothing but empty words on *the* page.

Nevertheless, spiritual burnout is a good place to be. In fact, you have to get there in order for you to receive what God truly has for your life. Jesus knew this when He gave the very first Beatitude in Matthew 5:3, "*Blessed are the poor in spirit, for theirs is the kingdom of heaven.*"

Therefore, if you're in spiritual burnout, praise God! Rejoice today, because something good is about to happen. Things are about to turn around. The Bible declares...

> *But those who wait on the LORD*
> *Shall renew their strength;*
> *They shall mount up with wings like eagles,*
> *They shall run and not be weary,*
> *They shall walk and not faint.* (Isaiah 40:31)

See, God isn't leaving you in this state of spiritual burnout. Nevertheless, you must get there in order to understand what Christ really did for you on the cross.

Look at it this way. People often wonder why they are experiencing a certain trial. They may even wonder if God made it happen. Rest assured, it isn't God's fault. His promises are true. God said He would meet our needs according to His riches in glory by Christ Jesus (Phil. 4:19).

So, if God isn't at fault, what is?

Causes of Spiritual Burnout

Burnout begins with a misconception of the Gospel. Sadly, many Christians view the Gospel as a formula. However, the Gospel isn't a formula; it's a relationship. The Gospel is centered around a person, Jesus, not a religious interpretation or understanding of the Bible. The Gospel is not a concept, a philosophy, or a way of living. The Gospel is centered on what Jesus accomplished on the cross two thousand years ago.

When you first came to Jesus and were saved, you were also filled with excitement. You probably remember that encounter, because of how it changed your life. You were so excited that you couldn't help but tell others and invite them to have the same encounter with Jesus that you did. Suddenly, you didn't care what people thought about you, because you were excited about Jesus.

This encounter happens countless times around the world as thousands of new Christians are born every day. However, somewhere along the line of their development, something tragic often happens. Instead of nurturing their relationship with Jesus, they turn to a formula, religion, in their attempts to live in victory.

Paul wrote:

> *But when the fullness of the time had come, God sent forth His Son, born of a woman, born under the law, to redeem those who were under the law, that we might receive the adoption as sons. And because you are sons, God has sent forth the Spirit of His Son into your hearts, crying out, "Abba, Father!"* (Gal. 4:4-6)

We understand that "Law" to be religion, one definition of which is, "a set of beliefs, values and practices." These beliefs, values and practices can quickly become bondage for people. In fact, we see this in the religious practices of Jesus' day. He was regularly condemned by the religious leaders for healing on the Sabbath, among other things. For them, even doing good was unacceptable on the Sabbath because it violated their interpretation of how to observe the day.

Jesus challenged their interpretation by saying that the Sabbath was created for man, not man for the Sabbath (Mark 2:27). His challenge infuriated the religious leaders because it undermined their control of the people.

Religion seeks to please God with works. Therefore, the Law defines our attempts to earn God's favor:

> *You shall not murder.*
> *You shall not commit adultery.*
> *You shall not steal.*
> *You shall not bear false witness against your neighbor.*
> *You shall not covet your neighbor's house; you shall not covet your neighbor's wife, nor his male servant, nor his female servant, nor his ox, nor his donkey, nor anything that is your neighbor's.* (Exodus 20:13-17)

These tenets of the Law define very important outward aspects of behavior; what is and is not acceptable in our dealings with others. However, to comply with this Law is difficult at best, and impossible at worst. Therefore, Christ came to set us free from the religious elements of the Law:

> *Therefore you are no longer a slave but a son, and if a son, then an heir of God through Christ. But then, indeed, when you did not know God, you served those which by nature are not gods. But now after you have known God, or rather are known by God, how is it that you turn again to the weak and beggarly elements, to which you desire again to be in bondage?* (Gal. 4:7-9)

No Longer Bound by Law

So, what happens?

Everything in life has rules. Your job has rules, and if you abide by those rules, you get paid. Likewise, there are rules about how fast you can drive on the roadways. If you disobey the rules, you will pay the consequences of a traffic ticket and fine. Obey the traffic laws and all is well.

Other examples include the rules in your home under which you were raised as a child. Rules helped define your boundaries and helped to keep you safe. They also helped you learn discipline and how to honor your father and mother.

So we grow up and live with a rules mentality. Sadly, we further translate that rules mentality into a form of religious righteousness to which we must conform in order to be accepted by God. For example:

- Pray one hour each day.
- Read the Bible through each year.
- Go to church every Sunday morning, Sunday evening and Wednesday evening.
- Put money in the offering.
- Be nice to everyone.

Now, on the surface, each of these "rules" seems like what we should do as Christians. However, grudgingly obeying out of obligation is worse than not obeying at all. Instead, these activities should spring out of our love for God and man instead of fear that He will reject us.

The truth is, these rules represent practices that demonstrate principles—honesty, truthfulness, integrity, loyalty, fidelity, etc. However, principles cannot be legislated by any law or enforced by any rule. Principles are internal, while practices are external. Religion seeks to legislate righteousness and to codify principled behavior through legalized practices or rules. However, religion falls short; principled behavior springs from the inside, not the outside.

Therefore, if we live our Christian life according to "Do this" or "Do that" we'll soon lose the excitement that marked our lives when we were first saved. We'll quickly burn out because we are unable to live according to burdensome rules.

Life in Christ

Remember our study in chapter 1 of *bios* and *zoe*? To quickly summarize, *bios* relates to the manner of how we live. It's our natural life that was given when we were born into this world. Whereas *zoe* refers to the life that God bestows on us in Christ. *Zoe* is His life in us, the Spirit of God in us quickening our life.

Jesus didn't come to give us a new formula for *bios* to follow. Jesus said: *"I have come that you may have life, and that they may have it more abundantly"* (John 10:10). The life to which Jesus is referring is *zoe*, life in Christ and Christ in us. *Zoe* is life as God lives it.

People work very hard trying to change their *bios*. They think that by doing so, their life will improve and things will be better. However, *bios* can't be changed enough to bring *zoe*. Any attempt to do so will always leave one frustrated and subsequently cause burnout.

While it's true that you can't change your *bios* into *zoe* you can exchange it. This is exactly what happens when you get saved, your *bios* is exchanged for *zoe*. When you receive Jesus, you don't have to work harder to be good, His righteousness is already in you.

Religion attempts to change *bios*, but lacks the strength and ability to do so. The Apostle Paul understood this well. He discovered that strength from the Lord only came in his weakness. Paul discovered *zoe*:

> *I have received wonderful revelations from God. But to keep me from getting puffed up, I was given a thorn in my flesh, a messenger from Satan to torment me and keep me from getting proud.*
>
> *Three different times I begged the Lord to take it away. Each time he said, "My gracious favor is all you need. My power works best in your weakness." So now I am glad to boast about my weaknesses, so that the power of Christ may work through me. Since I know it is all for Christ's good, I am quite content with my weaknesses and with insults, hardships, persecutions, and calamities.* **For when I am weak, then I am strong.** (2 Cor. 12:7-10 NLT emphasis added)

It Can't Be Done Alone

I remember several instances in my life when I felt like I couldn't make it. Though I tried, it seemed I was frustrated at every turn. Out of my frustration I cried out to God, saying, "I can't make it. I can't do it. I don't know how."

One time, *many* years ago, I lay down on my bed and told the Lord I couldn't go on. Desperately I cried out, "Jesus, I need You!" It seemed like I hadn't felt the presence of God for months, but as I cried out to God from my innermost being, His presence suddenly flooded over me. All I had to do was cry out to God.

When I try to achieve things in my flesh, I rarely succeed. However, when I cry out to God and say I need Him, He always responds. When I want to forgive those who have hurt me but don't know how, I cry out to God to help me. And He always does.

What I learned through this, I now share with you. Stop trying to make it alone! You can't do it on your own. You can't because, like me, you're weak. However, once you realize that you're weak, you can cry out to God and He will fill you with His strength.

Hang out with Jesus because you want to. This enables you to draw from His *zoe* (life). Abiding in Jesus produces the fruit of peace and joy. You'll be able to praise God because you are abiding in Jesus.

Choose Life–Choose Jesus

No religion exists that can change *bios* into *zoe*, but will instead leave you frustrated. Therefore, thank God you've not just received a new *bios*, but you've received the God life, *zoe*.

Then, when you begin to live outwardly as Christ lives inside of you, change will occur. Everything around you will change, and you'll begin doing things in response to *zoe* rather than obligation. Furthermore, because you have God's kind of life, you'll no longer have to struggle to keep the commandments of God.

You may be wondering how to get to that point. You can only get there through relationship with Jesus. He said, *"I am the way, the truth, and the life. No one comes to the Father except through Me"* (John 14:6). There is no other way to *zoe* but through Jesus. However, to have a relationship with Jesus, you must first meet Him.

You meet Jesus by receiving His love, and you receive His love upon understanding what He did for you on the cross. Jesus died so that you could have *zoe* (life). He bore all your sin and paid the penalty for you, so now all you have to do is accept His finished work. You don't have to work for it and you don't have to earn it. Just receive it.

God loves you far more than religion ever will. Furthermore, religion will never get you to God; only Jesus can do that (John 14:6). Therefore, if Jesus is the only way you can get to God, then it stands to reason that Jesus is also the only way to keep your faith in God. Religion is not the answer.

Religion enslaves you and holds you in bondage. However, Jesus sets you free. When Jesus lives in you, complete freedom is yours through His *zoe* kind of life.

So what will you choose? Are you ready to take hold of *zoe* and stop merely existing (*bios*)? If so, then take hold of Jesus. He's your answer. Pray this simple prayer to ask Him into your heart:

> *Jesus. I'm tired of merely existing. I want to live my life to the full, just like You promised I could in John 10:10. I give my life to You, Jesus, and invite You to live inside of me through Your Spirit. I ask Your forgiveness for all my sins and receive You now. Thank You, Jesus. Amen.*

I will not leave you nor forsake you.

—Josh 1:5b

In My Father's house are many mansions; if it were not so, I would have told you. I go to prepare a place for you. And if I go and prepare a place for you, I will come again and receive you to Myself; that where I am, there you may be also.

—John 14:2-3

7

Jesus' Covenant of Communion

"This meal, which we call 'Communion' or 'The Lord's Supper' is your time to reconnect with Jesus in remembrance of all that He's done for you. It's a time to recommit your life to Him, and to rededicate yourself to His service. This bread is a symbol...."

"Sally, do you understand what Pastor is saying about Communion?"

"Yes, I do understand. I feel excited, yet humbled at the same time. Is this normal when you do this or just because it's my first time?"

"Each time we partake of Communion our hearts are stirred, Sally. Just knowing what Jesus did on the cross is humbling, but knowing that the Lord's Supper connects us to Him in a special and unique way is both humbling and exciting. This never fades, but grows stronger each time as we pursue our relationship with Him."

To fully experience *zoe*, you must avail yourself of all that Christ has for you. Jesus' promise of abundant life (John 10:10b) is true, and He desires you to step into it at once.

One way to deepen your relationship with Jesus is through the Lord's Supper or Communion. Simple elements, bread and wine, represent for the Christian...

- the depth of God's love
- the fullness of Christ's sacrifice on the cross
- the extent to which He went to reach you
- His desire to internalize Himself in you

Power and strength are drawn from this simple, yet elegant, meal. Far more than a ritual, it's a life-giving experience for those who dare to plumb the depths of its meaning and purpose. Religion reduces this life-changing sacrament into a ritualized pattern, a form of godliness with no real meaning for everyday life. However, for those who seek to know Him, this meal represents an invitation to dine at the table of the King of glory.

The Covenant Meal

The Apostle Paul recognized the significance of this wonderful covenant meal. He wrote:

> *For I received from the Lord that which I also delivered to you: that the Lord Jesus on the same night in which He was betrayed took bread; and when He had given thanks, He broke it and said, "Take, eat; this is My body which is broken for you; do this in remembrance of Me." In the same manner He also took the cup after supper, saying, "This cup is the new covenant in My blood. This do, as often as you drink it, in remembrance of Me." For as often as you eat this bread and drink this cup, you proclaim the Lord's death till He comes. (1 Cor. 11:23-26)*

This covenant meal, communion or the Lord's Supper, is probably the most misunderstood sacrament in the church. This is especially true for evangelicals because we believe that our hearts are changed upon receiving Christ. When faced with a sacrament like the Lord's Supper, we tend to get a little nervous. So what does it mean to eat bread that represents the body of Jesus and drink wine that represents His blood?

After close study the Word of God, I've come to realize more than ever the tremendous importance of this covenant meal. I discovered that God has always dealt with people on the basis of covenant. Beginning with Adam, then Noah, Abraham, Moses, David and finally, Jesus, covenants form the basis for our communion with God. I came to understand that I'm in covenant with God through Christ Jesus, the same covenant that Jesus, the Son of Man, made with God the Father.

Covenants differ from contracts. A covenant forms a binding relationship until death, so they aren't simply entered into one day and cancelled the next. An example of this is the marriage covenant in which a man and woman are joined together in God, "till death do us part."

The Power of a Shared Meal

When parties enter into covenant, the occasion is often celebrated with a meal. This is perfectly illustrated by the wedding feast in the context of the marriage covenant. Something powerful happens when parties entering into agreement and then covenant eat together. A connection occurs that is uniquely suited to sharing a meal.

During the Last Supper on the eve of Jesus' crucifixion, He and the disciples were gathered in an upper room. The disciples were unaware of the events about to unfold, but Jesus knew and He wanted them to know as well. However, much more was about to happen than Jesus' arrest and subsequent execution, a new covenant was about to be instituted:

> *And as they were eating, Jesus took bread, blessed and broke it, and gave it to the disciples and said, "Take, eat; this is My body." Then He took the cup, and gave thanks, and gave it to them, saying, "Drink from it, all of you. For this is My blood of the new covenant, which is shed for many for the remission of sins."* (Matt. 26:26-28)

Jesus declared that His blood was the blood of a new covenant. Throughout history, when a covenant was established, blood was shed through a sacrifice. We see this with Adam, Noah, Abraham, Moses, David and now with Jesus. A new covenant was being established, bought and paid for by the blood of God's one and only Son, Jesus.

Jesus' words confused the disciples because they didn't know what was happening and misunderstood the meaning of what Jesus said. However, Jesus would not be deterred from what God had set for Him to do. Instead, He girded Himself with a towel and set about serving the disciples by washing their feet. The new covenant was about serving, not being served.

Do This in Remembrance...

Jesus told the disciples, and us, to eat this meal in remembrance of Him. By saying this, Jesus expressed the need for coming together to share the cup and break the bread with one another. But what purpose does this serve? Let's look at three:

Purpose # 1: "Do this in remembrance of Me."

We do this in remembrance of Christ. The covenant meal serves as a memorial by which we see the story of Jesus' sacrifice and relive the wonder of His love. Celebrating the covenant meal in remembrance of Christ helps us recall our testimony. We remember how Jesus...

- came into our lives and gave us the gift of life and righteousness.
- set us free when we were lost in our sin.
- healed us through His finished work on the cross.
- exchanged our need for His provision.
- delivered us from bondage to sin and wickedness.

Sadly, it's easy to forget what Jesus has done. Israel forgot her Redeemer, but we must never forget all that God has done for us. The covenant meal reminds us of all that Jesus has done.

When Jesus said, "Remember Me," we're to recall our testimony in Christ, when we met Jesus and we were saved. When we take the cup and the bread, we declare that we remember when we received Jesus Christ as Lord and Savior.

Remembrance reenacts what Jesus did. Taking the cup and the bread helps you recall how Jesus saved you when you were weak, bound in sin and headed for hell; how He brought you out of that miry clay and set your feet on the solid rock.

Scripture says that the saints overcome the enemy by the blood of the Lamb and the word of their testimony (Rev. 12:11). Testimony serves as the connection point between the saint and what happened to him or her in the Lord. Likewise, your testimony serves as your connection point in the Lord.

Some Christians live long lives, but become bitter and resentful, forgetful of what happened when Jesus saved them. For this reason, Jesus instituted the covenant meal by which to remember Him.

Partaking of the covenant meal brings to mind memories of what Jesus has done and enables you to stay on fire for Jesus. Recollection ensures you won't grow cold and become cynical because you won't remember what He has done for you.

Purpose #2: That we may be one, even as the Father and Jesus are one.

We celebrate the covenant meal because it declares our union with other believers. It declares that we are in Christ and Christ is in us.

We are united in a covenant based on unconditional love for God and one another, which is why the covenant meal is often referred to as *communion*. When we partake of the cup and the bread, instead of selfishness or insistence on being right we reinforce our love for one another.

Some Christians are afraid of being hurt and offended, so they opt to stay away from the church. However, we need other believers in order to express unconditional love. Any time we are offended or upset with another believer, we have an opportunity put love into action. If we never have relational challenges, we would have no opportunity to express unconditional love. The covenant meal serves as a powerful reminder of that love union.

The word *communion* means "fellowship" and "close connection." Paul said of this covenant meal, *"The cup of blessing which
we bless, is it not the communion of the blood of Christ? The bread
which we break, is it not the communion of the body of Christ?"* (1
Cor. 10:16).

Who Is the Body of Christ?

We are the body of Christ. We are in a relationship with one
another, not just with God. Paul said there is communion when
we partake of fellowship and by partaking of the bread and the
cup.

Paul encouraged the church in Corinth to cease having division
among them and to do nothing out of selfishness (1 Cor. 11:17-
23). Furthermore, he said that by eating and drinking the Lord's
Supper in an unworthy manner, they had not properly discerned
the Lord's body:

> *Therefore whoever eats this bread or drinks this cup of
> the Lord in an unworthy manner will be guilty of the
> body and blood of the Lord. But let a man examine
> himself, and so let him eat of the bread and drink of the
> cup. For he who eats and drinks in an unworthy manner
> eats and drinks judgment to himself, not discerning the
> Lord's body. For this reason many are weak and sick
> among you, and many sleep.* (1 Cor. 11:27-30)

Paul said that because they did not understand the nature of the
covenant of unconditional love, they were missing the entire
point of communion. Furthermore, this caused sickness and
even death among the people.

True unconditional love is not based on the loveliness of the person being loved, but upon the identity and attributes of God. In other words, unconditional love has nothing to do with what people do to you. Though you may be beaten and mistreated, unconditional love will prevail. That is the kind of love you are to have for your brothers and sisters in Christ.

If you are a recipient of God's love and in covenant with Him, then you must have a place in which to express and demonstrate that love of God. The natural place for this to occur is in the church where a union already exists between you and your brother in Christ. It's the territory where you exercise God's unconditional love. You are in Christ and Christ is in you. Likewise, Christ is in your brother and he is in Christ. Therefore, you are united in Christ.

Partaking of the bread and cup serves as a declaration that you are in communion with other believers. Therefore, if you are offended or hurt by a brother or sister in Christ, go talk to them. Doing otherwise moves you outside the covenant that God has made with you.

Reason #3: That we might know Him.

We celebrate the communion because it opens our eyes to see Christ and His Word. This is illustrated in Jesus' encounter with two disciples on the road to Emmaus (Luke 24:15-16,27-32,35). Jesus' preaching did not open the disciples' eyes to Him. Even though Jesus was there and spoke the truth, they didn't "see" Him.

We can remain unaware of Jesus' presence even though we hear the anointed Word preached. One reason why is not having blessed the bread—the body of Christ, our fellow believers. In other words, the covenant meal gives us an opportunity to bless (empower to succeed) our brothers and sisters in the Lord. When we bless our brothers and sisters, our eyes are open to the Lord, revealing the Word of God, which is often why miracles and healings take place. Revelation of the Word comes because we've blessed our brothers and sisters in Christ.

> *So it was, while they conversed and reasoned, that Jesus Himself drew near and went with them. But their eyes were restrained, so **that they did not know Him.***
>
> *And beginning at Moses and all the Prophets, He expounded to them in all the Scriptures the things concerning Himself.*
>
> *Then they drew near to the village where they were going, and He indicated that He would have gone farther. But they constrained Him, saying, "Abide with us, for it is toward evening, and the day is far spent." And He went in to stay with them. **Now it came to pass, as He sat at the table with them, that He took bread, blessed and broke it, and gave it to them. Then their eyes were opened and they knew Him;** and He vanished from their sight. And they said to one another, "Did not our heart burn within us while He talked with us on the road, and while He opened the Scriptures to us?"*
>
> *And they told about the things that had happened on the road, and how He was known to them in the breaking of bread.* (Luke 24:15-16, 27-32, 35)

Notice what happened in this incredible passage. Jesus was preaching the Word of God, but the eyes of the disciples were still not opened. They didn't recognize Jesus by His voice or by His preaching, but by the way He broke bread and prayed. Though Jesus was there with them teaching the Word of God, these disciples didn't recognize Him. Likewise, it's possible for you to be in a service where God is moving, but still be dead on the inside and feel nothing.

Jesus took the bread, His body, and blessed it. The bread represents Christ's body, which is also the church—you and me! We are a piece of the bread. Look at what Jesus did. First Jesus ministered the Word of God, then He took a piece of bread, His body (each disciple), and of Himself, blessed it and then gave it to them to eat.

To be *blessed* is to be empowered to succeed or to prosper. In other words, Jesus took His body, including you and me, and empowered it to prosper and be successful. It wasn't till then that these disciples had their eyes opened and saw Jesus as He is.

This is the point. If you want a revelation of who Jesus is, preaching will help you, but it's not enough. However, when you bless your fellow brothers and sisters, you empower them to prosper. When you bless the one who has offended you, spoken against you or whatever, you are given the ability to see Jesus for who He is.

You must bless the bread, Christ's body, if you want to...

- have a greater revelation of the truth of God.
- know Jesus the healer, Jesus the financial provider, Jesus the deliverer, Jesus the Savior, Jesus the Lord.
- walk in His truth and not just hear about it from a religious point of view.
- see Christ for who He really is.
- be in God's presence.

What Does This Have
to do With Communion?

Every time we take the bread, the body of Christ, we're to bless it, which empowers the body of Christ to succeed. We bless the body by praying for them and sowing seeds of goodness, seeds of love, and seeds of blessing. Then, we'll see Jesus as our personal Lord and healer as we partake of the communion.

The world has discovered the importance of forgiveness, something the church has been aware of for centuries. Nevertheless, unforgiveness runs rampant in today's world. A recent report on CNN concluded that countless lives are destroyed every year because of unforgiveness. Clearly, something must be done.

Something powerful occurs when we release the blessings of God through forgiveness. Just as God has forgiven us, we must forgive others:

> *If you forgive those who sin against you, your heavenly Father will forgive you. But if you refuse to forgive others, your Father will not forgive your sins.* (Matt. 6:14-15 NLT)

Forgiveness is paramount in our relationships. We must remember that we are inextricably linked together with our brothers and sisters in the Lord. We're part of the same body of Christ and linked together in the same covenant of unconditional love. Forgiveness is part of that love.

Motivated by God's unconditional love, we will look at our brothers and sisters with the desire to empower them to succeed. Then, when we take the bread and break it, we can pray: *"Oh, Lord God, thank You that Your body was broken so that Your body, the church, could be healed and made whole."* When we take the bread and bless them, we suddenly see Jesus the healer.

Partaking of the bread and cup is a very powerful sacrament. The act of blessing your brothers and sisters enables you to see Jesus the healer, which is very important if you are in need of healing. You can understand that Jesus' body was broken so yours doesn't have to be.

Seeking a financial miracle, you study the Word of God and memorize scriptures that promise prosperity. You begin declaring the promises found in God's Word and hope that God will respond. However, when you begin to bless the body of Christ and empower them, something happens on the inside. Suddenly, you begin to see Jesus the Provider and realize how He exchanged your poverty for His riches in glory. You begin to see how Jesus exchanged your shame for His acceptance.

In Remembrance of Him

Christ in you is powerful. His life, *zoe*, is yours for the living. For this, give thanks. Remember all the things that the Lord has done for you. Think of something in particular for which you are thankful. Do it in remembrance of what Jesus has done for you. Remember how Jesus...

- provided for you when you had nearly given up hope.
- touched your physical body and healed you when you were sick.
- restored your family.
- delivered you from sin and bondage.

As you remember what the Lord has done, pray this simple prayer of thanksgiving unto Him.

> *Thank You, Lord, that You've saved me. You've delivered me and set me free from the burden of sin. Thank You, Lord, for everything You've done for me. I thank You, Jesus. Amen*

"For by one offering He has perfected forever those who are being sanctified."

—Heb. 10:14

Chapter

Walk in the Blessing

For you were once darkness, but now you are light in the Lord. (Ephesians 5:8)

Someone once asked, "If I walk in the Spirit, why is it that I still sin?" Being filled with the Spirit is an ongoing process of being filled over and over again. And, being sanctified is a process of growth.

We live in a microwave world in which everyone wants instant solutions. After all, television solves crimes or family problems in one hour, why can't we? Truthfully, *life* doesn't work that way. Life's journey as we are led by the Spirit is filled with lessons, steps forward and backwards, ups and downs and many trials. Nonetheless, we are being perfected as we walk in the Spirit because we were perfected at the cross. How were we perfected? Through Christ's sacrifice, we were put in a position to receive the blessings and promises of God by faith in *life.*

Christ has already perfected us. This means that we are already made complete—filled with liberty from sin and filled with the power to live for Christ. We have been made complete because of what Jesus accomplished for us on the cross.

We don't have to pay for our sin, or our sickness, or our disease or our problems anymore because Jesus provided for us. One offering was made, and the offering that was made was sufficient for all our needs. He has done it. We don't have to do it. We have been perfected. We are the righteousness of God in Christ Jesus. We are blessed by God. Why?

Because Jesus lives on the inside. Greater is He who is in me than he who is in the world; Christ in you, the hope of glory. Christ lives on the inside of us. It is because of His offering that we have received eternal life. We must get that revelation into our spirit man. We must have a revelation of the cross of Christ.

But at the same time it says here, "For by one offering you have been made perfect." Or, He has perfected forever those who are being sanctified. In other words, He has already made you perfect, but at the same time there is a process, which is both future and present tense.

So, in one tense, we have what He has done, and at the same time, we have what we must do. *Sanctified* means "to be set apart as holy before God." You see, God wants us to walk in holiness. It is one thing to understand what we have received. It is another thing to understand that God wants us to walk holy.

Your Position in Christ

Ephesians also describes what we have received in Christ Jesus. Ephesians 2 declares that we are seated with Christ Jesus in the heavenly places far above all principalities and powers. We are

seated with Christ Jesus. We are not seated just a little bit over
the powers of darkness that are just under our feet. No! We are
seated with Christ Jesus far above–far above.

Then two chapters later in Ephesians 4 we are encouraged to
walk in love, *walk* in unity, *walk* in wisdom and *walk* in the
light. So, even though we have received positional sanctification,
experientially we must still walk in holiness, obedience and sanctification. Sanctification in Christ is a gift; we cannot earn holiness. Through the cross, we receive the power in the Holy Spirit
to obey God and do what He requires.

> *He has shown you, O man, what is good;*
> *And what does the LORD require of you*
> *But to do justly,*
> *To love mercy,*
> *And to walk humbly with your God?* (Micah 6:8)

How is it possible to do what God requires? Through the cross,
we have been justified through the blood of Christ to receive His
impartation of holiness. We have also received the gift of the
Holy Spirit (Acts 2:38) so that we can walk in holiness.

Let me give you an example. Suppose you have a lamp which is
plugged in but not turned on. The power is there. The potential
for light is there. But until the switch is thrown, no light issues
forth. The same is true of *zoe* (*life*) which is sanctified through
Christ. Through faith in Jesus the Christ, we are plugged in
(positional sanctification) to His righteousness and holiness.
But, we must walk in obedience (experiential sanctification) by
turning on the switch (obeying His truths).

Through the cross of Christ, we have the promise and impartation of holiness because the risen Jesus has given us His Holy

Spirit (Acts 1-2). The promise of the Holy Spirit becomes a reality when we trust Jesus as Lord and Savior (Acts 2:38). The power to walk in the Spirit comes with the responsibility to walk in holiness: *"Therefore, having these promises, beloved, let us cleanse ourselves from all filthiness of the flesh and spirit, perfecting holiness in the fear of God"* (2 Cor. 7:1).

Legally, we are joint heirs with Christ Jesus, but experientially we need to walk in the reality of it. The problem is that what happens in church, so often, is that we try to begin to walk experientially in the blessings of God before we have had a revelation of what He has done for us.

It's strange. According to religion, we first start with walking. We say, "This is what you need to do first. And if you do this, if you walk righteously, if you do the right thing, if you walk in unity, if you walk in love, if you do all these things that we must do, then you will somehow or other be seated with Christ Jesus."

But no, it doesn't start there. It starts with being seated with Christ Jesus. It starts with having a revelation. The book of Ephesians begins with, "I pray for you that your hearts will be enlightened to the truth of the Word of God, that you are seated with Christ Jesus in the heavenly places, that once you were dead, but you have been made alive through Christ Jesus, and that He lives on the inside of you" (Author's paraphrase. Read Eph. 1:15-21).

The life of God starts with that revelation. It does not start with, "This is what you must do. Follow these 'Forty Rules of Proper Church Behavior.' Or, follow these 'Forty Rules on How to Be a Christian.'"

Zoe life cannot be lived that way. We are just defeating ourselves. No amount of trying will ever be able to get us to the point where we will walk righteously before God. We can't do it. It's just impossible.

So, life (*zoe*) begins with having a revelation of Christ. It begins in knowing Him and having an understanding of what He has done for us. But then, as we move along in our lives and now have Christ living on the inside of us, now we learn to walk as Christ walks.

How Do We Walk in God's Blessings?

Although much could be shared on this subject, there are two basic steps for walking in the Spirit's blessings for your life.

Step 1: Walk in faith.
We must learn to walk by faith. The Apostle Paul says that Christ has redeemed us from the curse of the law so that the blessing of Abraham might come upon us and that we might receive the promise of the Spirit **through faith**. (Gal. 3:14) So many biblical passages reveal incredible truths about faith:

The just shall live by faith. (Gal. 3:11)

I have been crucified with Christ; it is no longer I that live, but Christ that lives in me. Therefore, the life that I now live, I live by faith in the Son of God. (Gal. 2:20)

For we walk by faith, not by sight. (2 Cor. 5:7)

For whatever is born of God overcomes the world. And this is the victory that has overcome the world — our faith. (1 John 5:4-5)

> *For I say, through the grace given to me, to everyone who is among you, not to think of himself more highly than he ought to think, but to think soberly, as God has dealt to each one a measure of faith.* (Rom. 12:3-4)

> *He did not waver at the promise of God through unbelief, but was strengthened in faith, giving glory to God, and being fully convinced that what He had promised He was also able to perform.* (Rom. 4:20-22)

> *For in it the righteousness of God is revealed from faith to faith; as it is written, "The just shall live by faith."* (Rom. 1:17)

Faith is the victory that overcomes the world. There is no other way to walk than through faith. If we don't walk by faith, we will be defeated.

Imagine for a moment two parallel worlds separated by a barrier. The one world is called the kingdom world, i.e., the spiritual world. The other world is the natural world in which we exist.

The natural world is captured and viewed with our natural senses. It's everything we see with our physical eyes. The spiritual world or the Kingdom of God world can only be viewed through the help of the Holy Spirit. It can be a simple revelation of Christ in our hearts, or through a vision, a dream, the inner voice of the Spirit or even a prophetic utterance.

We enter this world when the canvases of our hearts are painted with the picture of God. It could happen as we spend time with Christ in prayer or while we hear the Gospel being preached, or even during worship when our hearts connect with Christ. Our hearts are filled with a joy and peace as we catch a glimpse of God's plan and purpose for our lives.

Where many miss God's plans and purposes is not in the ability to enter this spiritual world. But it's how to bring that world of God's Kingdom into the natural realm. For example, we participate in an incredible service or prayer meeting where the presence of God is so tangible, and then we return home with such joy and peace in our hearts. It's like heaven on earth.

But soon thereafter, we encounter the barrier between the spiritual and the natural. Unfavorable circumstances and people appear. Suddenly there is a struggle between what God has poured into our hearts and what we face in the natural realm. How do we break through the barrier that exists between these two worlds and bring what we have experienced in the spiritual world into the physical world?

We break through the barrier with the most effective battering ram we have—even our faith! "Faith comes by hearing and hearing by the word of God" (Rom. 10:17).

Abraham is an example of this. God revealed to him the plan of God for his life through visions and dreams. Through the help of stars and sand, Abraham's heart was painted with a dream from God which seemed impossible. He was to be a father of nations and multitudes, so large he could not even count his offspring.

Perhaps Abraham and Sarah took many strolls at night gazing into the sky, counting the stars and visualizing their great family. They had heard from God. They had entered that spiritual world–the Kingdom of God. They had seen what was impossible by natural means.

However, they would awaken every morning with no evidence of the promise. I'm sure the people around them, just like the people around us, wondered if God's promises were really true. Perhaps they questioned if Abraham and Sarah had really heard from God. Perhaps the neighbors whispered.

Of course, Abraham would have been bombarded with the realities of the natural world. For years, there was nothing—no baby! Time was running out in the natural. Then, one day Isaac was born. He was the beginning of the fulfillment of the promise of God.

What was it that caused that which God had shown Abraham in the spiritual realm to manifest in the natural? Paul says in Romans 4:18-20:

> *Who, contrary to hope, in hope* **believed,** *so that he became the father of many nations,* **according to what was spoken, "So shall your descendants be."** *And not being weak in* **faith**...*he did not waver at the promise of God through unbelief, but was strengthened in faith giving glory to God (Emphasis added.)*

Abraham held onto the promise of God. That's what faith is–holding onto the promises of God, when you are faced with the barrier that separates the spiritual world from the natural. When all the pressure comes as you move through the barrier, hold on to what God has declared. Abraham did not waver, he held on to the promise.

That's why it's so important to deposit the Word of God into your spirit man. Listen to the Word of God and don't be led by the voice of your emotions. That's the voice of the natural world when your flesh cries out, "Oh, the circumstances are over-

WALK IN THE BLESSING

whelming me! I don't know what to think. I don't know what to do. I am ready to give up. I don't know what to do."

By faith enter the spiritual world of God's Kingdom that is based on God's Word. It is based upon what God has said…what God has declared…what God is saying to us today. The kingdom world is a superior world to the natural world.

What Is Faith? *Faith is listening to the Word of God and refusing to yield to the voice of feelings.* Hebrews 11:1 talks about how faith is the substance of things hoped for, the evidence of things not seen. The world was framed by the Word of faith.

Hebrews 11 narrates stories about the heroes of faith. They were those who throughout history refused to believe the voice of circumstances and who refused to listen to the voice of feelings. But they would tap into the Word of God and allow the Word of God to be number one in their lives. They made decisions based upon what the Word of God said, not based upon what their feelings said.

When Abraham's son Isaac grew into a young man, God commanded Abraham to sacrifice his only son. Often when God says something, it makes no sense. Our logic says, "This is not right, God, because in order for me to be that father of multitudes, in order for this nation to come from me, I need to keep my baby. And You want me to sacrifice my baby?"

God says, "Yes. That's what I want you to do."

Abraham listened to the Word of God instead of listening to the voice of his feelings. And if you are going to live a victorious life in Christ Jesus…if you want to live with the blessings of God upon your life, you must learn to listen to the Word of God and not listen to the circumstances of life and the problems of life. Don't look at your pocketbook every day and get discouraged. Put it away and say, "God, I am just going to trust You because whatever I am doing right now is not working anyhow. I'm going to trust You and trust Your Word."

Faith is also obeying promptly what God says. If you take time to listen to your feelings, and if you take time consulting with others about what they think, then you will substitute procrastination for obedience.

If we are to break through the barrier between the natural and the spiritual realm, then we will have to obey promptly. If we don't obey the Word of God, the longer we wait, the less likely we will do it. Remember this: Disobedience gives Satan a foothold and strengthens the barrier or wall between us and God's kingdom. Obeying God shatters the barriers between us and His Kingdom, His promises and His promises for our lives.

Step 2: Guard Your Tongue!

The second step is linked to the first one. Paul exhorts us in 2 Corinthians 4:13, *"And since we have the same spirit of faith, according to what is written, 'I believed and therefore I spoke,' we also believe and therefore speak."*

Perhaps the biggest problem among those desiring to walk in God's blessings is the problems created by their tongues. James 3:2 says, *"For we all stumble in many things. If anyone does not stumble in word, he is a perfect man, able also to bridle the whole body."*

All of us have problems with our tongues. We allow curses to be spoken that we don't even know about. The Bible says that we are snared by the words that we speak. We want the blessings of God; we want to walk in holiness, but we have been telling ourselves it can't be done. No wonder it can't happen! It is not God's problem. The problem lies with the words we use. We moan and groan. We enjoy complaining.

If we are to maintain the incredible life we have through Christ, we must guard our tongue. The devil cannot defeat us; the world cannot defeat us; we are only defeated by the words we use.

As God called people out of Egypt, He had prepared the Promised Land of blessings for them. The wilderness was not much of an upgrade from Egypt. There are times believers feel as though life with Christ is not much of an upgrade from what they used to have before they were born again. The initial joy of having been released from the bondage of Egypt has quickly faded. The wilderness has no real charm. Why is it we get stuck in the wilderness of spiritual emptiness?

Our words determine our future. For example, as soon as Moses had led Israel out of Egypt, he immediately endeavored to move the people into the Promised Land. He sent twelve spies to prepare for immediate advancement into the land that flowed with milk and honey.

Two of them, Joshua and Caleb, returned with faith in the heart and declared, *"Let us go up at once and take possession; for we are well able to overcome it"* (Num. 13:30).

The other ten had a different report, "We are not able to go up against the people, for they are stronger than we" (v. 31).

One chapter later, God responded to their words: *"Just as you have spoken in My hearing, so I will do to you...Except for Caleb, the son of Jephunneh and Joshua the son of Nun, you shall by no means enter the land which I swore I would make you dwell in"* (Num. 14:28, 30).

If we are to walk in the blessings of God, we must be set free from our tongue disease! Jesus said we will give an account for every idle word spoken. An idle word is a word spoken carelessly, without premeditation. There are many words that we can eliminate. Common idle, destructive words spoken by our tongues such as, "It's driving me crazy." Or, "I just can't take it anymore. You are good for nothing around here."

Whenever we tell our kids they are good for nothing, we are cursing them. We impede empowerment in that child's life. That negative word has to be revoked. Perhaps your parents have spoken words over your life that are curse words rather than words of blessing. Those words have to be revoked in the name of Jesus.

Some get sick and wonder why they are sick all of the time. Perhaps it is the consequence of the words, "I am so sick and tired," or "Sickness runs in my family." Refuse to speak such idle and negative words! By His blood, you have received redemption from every sickness and every disease! Jesus took upon Himself your infirmities and bore your sicknesses.

Some people say, "Well, you know, I can never make ends meet. My dad was just the same. We just are miserably poor, destitute and broke. Give me a handout, and I will be happy." Then they ask, "Why are the blessings of God not coming for me?" They are cursed by their own words.

"My mother told me that my husband would leave me." No wonder breakups in families and family alienations occur when words like that are spoken. Don't ever say such a thing! Refuse to have an unbridled tongue. Negative words like a fire will consume you and others. Refuse to speak curses. Speak the Word of God.

Take these important practical and spiritual steps right now:

- Don't listen to your circumstances.
- Don't listen to your negative situation.
- Don't listen to the negative voices around you.
- Stand on God's Word!
- If the Word of God says it, then declare it! What you say with your mouth will determine your future!

If we speak the Word of God, we speak *life*. If our words agree with the Gospel, the blessings of life are ours.

Rather than declaring destructive, lifeless words that lead to death, speak words of life that will change your environment.

Decide to Walk in Blessing

You can make a decision for life, for *zoe,* right now! First, walk by faith. Trust God with your destiny. Believe His promises for your life.

Secondly, decide to bridle your tongue. Speak life, **not** death. Declare God's promises over your life and the lives of those around you. Stop making idle, negative comments and threats.

I invite you to pray this now:

Oh, Father, I come before You. I humble myself before You. I repent, Lord, for idle words that I have spoken over my life, and over the lives of my family, friends and associates at work.

I repent for speaking curses over our families, over our jobs, over our lives, over the church and over one another. Father, I ask that You would purge me, and Lord, that You would take that live coal from the altar and put it on my tongue. As Isaiah came into Your presence, and he became undone, and he declared, "Woe is me, for I have sinned."

Father, You reached down for the coal and touched his lips. I ask, dear God, that You would bring that coal, and that You would touch my lips, that You would cleanse my tongue. I ask, Lord, that I would no longer speak words of cursing, but Father, that I would release blessing.

Oh, thank You, Father.

Right now, in the name of Jesus, I take authority over every curse that has been spoken over my life, over the lives of my family, over the lives of my community and over the lives of my church. I revoke every curse-filled word spoken in the name of Jesus. I revoke it now, in Jesus mighty name! Amen.

Final Word

Choose Life!

Therefore choose life, that both you and your descendants may live; that you may love the LORD your God, that you may obey His voice, and that you may cling to Him, for He is your life and the length of your days. (Deut. 30:19b-20a)

I invite you to embrace life and walk in the fullness of God's blessings for you. If you have further questions about real life in Jesus Christ or how to walk in the fullness of His blessings for you, please contact our ministry so that we can minister to you and pray for you.

May God richly bless you with a full life in Jesus Christ, from the *inside out!*

I want to pray for you now. I invite you to pray my prayer for you out loud and more than once as you live *life from the inside out!*

Father, in the name of Jesus, I ask You to reveal Your incredible love to everyone who reads this book. May each one encounter the greatness of what You accomplished on the cross for us, and may the eyes of their hearts be enlightened to Your mercy and compassion for them. From this moment on live through them, and may Christ be seen in them in all that they do. In Jesus' wonderful name! Amen.

Index

Ministry Information

We want to pray with you, provide you with resources for living inside out and hear from you. Contact us at:

David Youngren
Harvest International Ministries
P.O. Box 37
Oshawa, ON L1H 7K8
Canada
www.davidyoungren.org